Margaret
Princess
of Hungary

S.M.C.

With a Preface by
Benet O'Driscoll, O.P.

2013
DNS Publication

Margaret, Princess of Hungary by S.M.C. was originally published in London in 1945 by Blackfriars Publications. A Second Edition was published in 1954. This 2013 edition by DNS Publications contains the original text of the Second Edition.

Copyright © 1954 SMC

Printed in the United States of America

Nihil obstat: H. Franciscus Davis, S.T.D.
Censor deputatus.
Imprimatur: Thomas,
Archiepiscopus Birminamiensis.
Birmingamiae die 12a Februarii 1945.

All rights reserved. No part of this book may be reproduced, stored in a retrieval system, or transmitted in any form, or by any means, electronic, mechanical, photocopying, or otherwise, without the prior written permission of the publisher or the congregation of the English Dominican Sisters of Saint Catherine of Siena, except by a reviewer, who may quote brief passages in a review.

Dominican Nuns of Summit
543 Springfield Avenue
Summit, New Jersey 07901
www.nunsopsummit.org

ISBN: 1480089257
ISBN-13: 978-1480089259

Books by the Same Author

A Treasure of Joy and Gladness

And No Birds Sing

Angel of the Judgment

As the Clock Struck Twenty

Brother Petroc's Return

Children Under Fire

The Chronicles of Thomas Frith, O.P.

The Dark Wheel

The Flight and the Song

Henry Suso: Saint and Poet

Jacek of Poland

Margaret, Princess of Hungary

Once in Cornwall

The Spark in the Reeds

Steward of Souls

Storm out of Cornwall

Contents

Preface 1

Chapter One 9

Chapter Two 21

Chapter Three 43

Chapter Four 63

Chapter Five 83

Chapter Six 99

Chapter Seven 121

Chapter Eight 139

Chapter Nine 161

Chapter Ten 185

About the Author 197

Preface

It is not without its significance that, in the midst of a war that threatened civilization and at a time when Rome was in danger of destruction, the Holy See should have concerned itself with the canonization of a contemplative nun who died at an early age seven centuries ago, who during her short lifetime did nothing the world would call great. The Church is primarily concerned with what is divine and eternal. The circumstances attending the birth and religious vocation of Princess Margaret of Hungary witness to the different standard by which men then lived, and are a challenge to the world today, just as the life of the Saint is a challenge to this luxury-loving age. Hungary had been overwhelmed by Mongol invaders, and Western Europe was in deadly peril. Modern warfare could add little to the horror and desolation caused by the savage hordes who pillaged and destroyed at will. It was then that King Bela, to implore the divine help for his country, solemnly dedicated his unborn child to the service of God and St Dominic. The immediate causes of the liberation that followed at once, can be traced and studied, but no one can fail to see in them the finger of God's over-ruling Providence.

The Saint is one who loves God intensely. There is in truth but one way to sanctity, the following of him who said: I am The Way. Yet diversity of character, circumstance and tradition make absolute uniformity unthinkable, and the lives of the Saints show the myriad ways in which the life of our Lord has been reproduced and great union with God achieved. Religious Orders have their own traditions of spirituality, resulting partly from the special purpose which called each Order into being and the choice of means that necessitated, partly from the permanent impress of the character of the founder, and in part perhaps by the influence of generations who have striven to keep the spirit and letter of the rule.

Margaret entered the Dominican convent at Veszprim within twenty-five years of the death of St Dominic, at a time when the influence of the founder might be expected to be still at its strongest. It should cause no surprise that her spiritual life was stamped with an asceticism that was so marked a characteristic of the life of St Dominic himself. Indeed asceticism has ever been one of the traits in Dominican spirituality, and the lives of such Saints as Louis Bertrand, Rose of Lima and Blessed Henry Suso best exemplify the tendency.

Theologians in the abstract way of their science discuss the purpose of asceticism as a help to more intense love of God. It is a means of training the will and forming character, of attaining that mastery of self without which no one can for long give time, thought and energy to the love and service of God, or be prepared should the need arise to give up and sacrifice all rather than offend God. But it is also the great means of removing the obstacle to union with God which results from sin, making satisfaction, as it does to God's Holiness and Justice for the outrage which sin offered. At its simplest satisfaction means that we who followed our own will even when it meant offending God, now seek to repair the outrage to his Majesty by generously accepting in reparation and love something that goes against our will. The need for satisfaction is little understood today, yet it is surely one of the principal lessons of the Incarnation and Redemption that God in his ineffable Holiness and Infinite Justice looks for reparation for sin. To say that God hates sin and looks for satisfaction is to do no injury to his limitless Mercy, for in him—in a way that here below we cannot fathom or understand—Infinite Mercy and Infinite Justice are identified.

But whatever abstract reasonings may influence the theologian, we maybe sure that in the concrete a soul such as Margaret's was influenced rather by a burning devotion to the Passion of our Lord, as was St Dominic before her. Her precocious devotion to the Crucifix pointed the direction in which her spiritual life would develop. Two other factors undoubtedly influenced the course of her spiritual growth. She knew that before birth she had been dedicated as an expiatory victim to secure the salvation of her country, and also she was conscious of a tendency, disruptive of religious life, to treat her with special consideration because of her royal birth. She began a way of life which to those unacquainted with the lives of the Saints must seem inhuman and even repulsive. To an utterly heroic degree she practiced the austerities of fasting, deprivation of sleep, exhausting menial work, and other bodily penance. To these she added a penance and humiliation perhaps more galling than any, that of extreme neglect in her personal habits. It may seem strange that one so innocent should have led a life of this terrifying self-immolation, but she knew that her sinless Lord made expiation for the sins of the world, and she could not forget that she was herself a victim of expiation for her people.

The consuming love of God which inspires the Saints prevents them from being one-sided, no matter how extreme may seem their practice of one virtue. In the natural order great prudence, courage, or any other virtue, may result from natural bent of character and be without due counterpoise, but on the supernatural plane it is otherwise. The growth of all the infused virtues is proportionately the same. In a really supernaturalized life any heroic practice of virtue is normally accompanied by the exercise, also to an heroic degree, of virtues which are in appearance most opposite. In Margaret the almost inhuman penances and the fatigue which they brought were accompanied by an angelic sweetness of manner and an entire forgetfulness of self, a love for the poor which is the authentic sign of the disciple of Christ.

Such was the life of one whom the Church has inscribed in the Calendar of Saints seven centuries after her death. There is much in her life that we are not called upon to imitate, but if the world is to be cured from its present ills it must return to the standards by which she lived.

BENET O'DRISCOLL, O.P.

Chapter One

The year of our Lord 1271 was a notable one in the annals of the Kingdom of Hungary. Everywhere, people were declaring that the glory of the Arpads had been renewed, and that the great days of Saint Stephen their first Christian King had returned to the country. Now this new luster which had been shed on the great Arpad dynasty was in no way resultant from the reign of that most unhappy monarch, Stephen V—half pagan himself, with a wholly pagan wife even though she had been baptized a Christian before her marriage—who was now hastening to his grave amid the turmoil of civil war. It was with the fame of his sister that the whole country-side was ringing; his younger sister, Margaret, a Dominican nun, who had just died at the age of twenty-eight years, twenty-four of which had been spent in the Priories of Veszprim and Saint Mary of the Isle. And, stranger still, this young girl had done nothing of any great note during the twenty-eight years of her life; she had not even been Prioress in her own convent, the house which her royal father had built specially for her. In fact, during the last ten of those years, beyond her earnest prayers for its welfare, she had had absolutely no connection with the political life of her country.

Her own community had loved her dearly, no one could help loving one who was always so gentle, so kind, so unselfish; and yet quite a number of the nuns had been a little ashamed of her, for she had always been so untidy and unkempt, in a dirty patched habit, and even her hands and face were often far from clean. What was worse, she insisted on going to the grille to see her relations and their friends, the highest and noblest in the land, just as she was; and the sisters could never persuade her to change her disreputable habit for something more seemly. She really might have been a swineherd's daughter instead of a royal princess. She must have had a reason for what she did, she was always so consistent in her refusal to make any change; but what that reason might be many of them could not fathom.

When she died early in the year, some of them had been surprised to find how bitterly they had wept. While she was still alive they had not realized how much they had loved her. But they knew now how terribly they were missing her; missing her helpfulness and her lovely smile. She had always somehow been just on the spot where she was needed, where there was work to be done, or where there was someone sick, sad, or merely cross. Half a dozen were now needed to do what she had done alone and with such joyful alacrity.

Tales were finding their way into the convent, tales of miracles that their little sister was working; wonderful cures, and other extraordinary answers to prayer. Now the nuns came to think of it, she used to work miracles and obtain numerous favors for them inside the enclosure while she was still alive; but she had always been so simple and matter-of-fact about it all that they had scarcely noticed anything unusual in what she was doing; it was just Margaret. Since her death she had shown her power far more widely, and wonderful tales were pouring in from all sides.

Her own community, it is true, had received many favors at her hands since her death, but they had expected this somehow, for they had always gone to Margaret so freely while she was alive that it was only natural to appeal to her now when her power was still greater, and her benevolence was certainly not lessened.

She had only been dead a few hours when she first showed her own sisters that she had not forgotten them. The Prioress, Sister Catherine, was greatly distressed to find that a severe headache from which she had been suffering for six days was so increasing in violence that there seemed no hope for her being present at Sister Margaret's Dirge. She had had considerable experience of Sister Margaret while she was alive, and so she turned to her now, asking God that through the merits of his servant, she might be cured. The headache went immediately, and she resumed all her duties next day.

Little Sister Elizabeth, Sister Margaret's own niece, the daughter of King Stephen, had a very painful sore throat, so swollen that she could neither eat nor speak. When the Vigil of the Assumption came round and she was still voiceless, she was greatly disappointed to think that she would be unable to sing our Lady's Office. So, after Compline, remembering the aunt who had loved the Blessed Virgin so dearly, she crept away to her tomb, to lay her aching throat and head on the marble shrine. It was a strange sensation to feel warmth and healing creeping back through her veins, but it thrilled her to find that she was able to sing Matins with a full voice.

Sister Catherine, the Chantress, had such a sore throat during Lent that she was unable to carry out her Choir duties. On the Wednesday in Holy Week she followed Sister Elizabeth's example, and went to Sister Margaret's tomb. She left the shrine perfectly cured and was able to sing Tenebrae that night.

As news continued to pour in of the miracles which were being worked in the country round through the intercession of the Saint, and there was talk of petitioning the Pope for the canonization of the Hungarian Princess, the nuns, who knew that they would be called on to witness at the Process, began to gather together in an orderly fashion all that they could remember of Sister Margaret; little ordinary things, many of them, but for that very reason instinct with life.

One of their number was very desirous of testifying to Margaret's sanctity, and so she was correspondingly disappointed to find that she had nothing further to add to what many of them were already prepared to say. She went to the grille in the Choir whence she could see the tomb, and there she asked her little Sister to gratify her desire, and show her something about which she might give testimony. As she prayed, a paralyzed woman was carried in, and on touching the tomb she was immediately cured.

In the meantime, well authenticated stories were accumulating, of which the following may serve as specimens.

A coach maker from the village of Dan had been so completely paralyzed that the sinews of his legs had contracted until his knees touched his chest. He was carried on pilgrimage to Saint Margaret's tomb, where he lay praying for a week. At the end of that time, while Mass was being celebrated, he suddenly rose, and walked three times round the tomb. He was completely and permanently cured.

The father of a family in the town of Bissenen in Albania had lost his sight. A visit to the Saint's tomb proved fruitless; but on his return, having offered his act of resignation, he made his wife open the shutters of the darkened room, and straightway he saw.

Many possessed persons on being brought to the shrine were freed from the power of the devil. The young king, Ladislaus, when at the point of death, was cured by the application of the Saint's veil to his head and chest.

A pagan was converted with his whole family, after his horse which had been blinded in one eye recovered its sight through the intercession of the Saint.

So the list of cures continually mounted up. Their number is prodigious; the blind, the lame, the paralyzed, those possessed by devils, lunatics, afflicted persons of all kinds have obtained a complete cure at the tomb of the Hungarian Wonderworker. Her Cause has been brought before the Holy See several times. It was opened at Rome in 1275, four years after her death; in 1409, Blessed John Dominici, of her own Order, Apostolic Legate in Germany, granted an Indulgence of forty days to all who should visit her tomb. Mathias Corvinus, King of Hungary, pressed the Holy See for her canonization in 1464. The hearing of the Cause was resumed in 1640, but was never completed. In the eighteenth century, the relics of the Saint were destroyed by revolutionaries. Pope Pius VI consented to her veneration as a Saint, and Pope Pius VII extended the privilege of celebrating her feast to the whole Dominican Order.

In November 1943, Pius XII by special decree declared her a canonized Saint. In the decree her life is summed up as one of uninterrupted exercise of prayer, penance, and work for her country and for the Church.

Ordinary, unimportant folk will find comfort and inspiration in learning how, when the whole of her life was spent in the cloister, Saint Margaret carried out an apostolate which was worldwide.

Chapter Two

History presents us with many insoluble problems, not the least among them being the question as to the motive power which underlies the migration of savage tribes and races; on the face of it the whole thing seems haphazard, and yet, nothing merely fortuitous would recur over and over again as this has done. From the fourth to the thirteenth centuries, horde after horde of barbarians, actuated by some strange impulse, surged out from Asia, leaving its huge open spaces and scanty population, into Europe which was according to contemporary ideas already sufficiently populated. In waves they poured in, and it seemed as if nothing could stop them. Hungary, which afterwards became the eastern bulwark of Europe, was herself peopled by successive races of barbarians from the east; first the Vandals, then the Huns, and lastly, towards the end of the ninth century, the Magyars who are the forefathers of the Hungarians of today.

These Magyars were themselves related to the Huns, and they were cognizant of the fact, for they called their distinctive dress, a tunic covered with rich embroideries, Attila. They came from the banks of the Ural River, on the borderland between Europe and Asia, under a famous warrior, Arpad by name. His sons and their descendants succeeded him, first as tribal leaders, and later, when the nomad bands had turned farmers and settled permanently in the country, they took the office and title of King. Hungary, lying in the rich, fertile plain of the Danube, was precisely the type of country to appeal to nomads with flocks and herds, and so they settled down as a race of husbandmen.

At the end of the tenth century, the Magyar King, Stephen, became a Christian, and his people followed him. He became the first Saint of the Arpad dynasty, which was conspicuous no less for the number of Saints that it gave to the Church than for the power and courage of its rulers. Among the earlier Saints, after Saint Stephen himself, there came Saint Ladislaus, and Saing Imre. Saint Hedwig was the sister of Saint Margaret's grandmother, and Saint Elizabeth, widow of the Landgraf of Thuringia, was her father's sister. Among her own sisters, Saint Cunegunde married Boleslaus the Chaste, King of Poland, and after his death became a Poor Clare in the convent at Sandecs. Iolanthe, who married Boleslaus the Pious of Poland, followed Cunegunde as a Poor Clare, and was beatified, while Constance married Danilovich, Prince of Halitsch, and was a Dominican Tertiary. Although the latter has not been honored by public cults, she also has been called Blessed by the voice of the people. Saint Louis, Bishop of Toulouse, was the son of Margaret's brother, Stephen V.

Very early in the history of the Dominican Order, Friars Preachers came to Hungary; for during the second General Chapter held at Bologna Saint Dominic himself sent Paul of Hungary, and Blessed Sadoc to found the Province of Pannonia, and thus his sons realized their Father's ambition of preaching to the Cumans. Both of them won the martyrs' Crown. Blessed Sadoc was slain by the Tartars together with forty-eight of his brethren in the Priory he had founded at Sandomir in Poland, and of which he was Prior.

From very early days, Hungary was of particular importance to the Dominicans, since it was a convenient starting point for missionary journeys to the east. The sending of missions from Hungary was still further facilitated by the special love and kindness which both the king and his subjects showed to the sons of Saint Dominic.

King Andreas, father of Bela IV and grandfather of Saint Margaret, a strange mixture of piety and recklessness, at one time preparing for a Crusade, and at another lying under sentence of excommunication, was convinced of the truth of popular legends concerning a portion of the Magyar race which was reputed to have remained behind in Asia Minor when the rest of the tribe migrated to Hungary. So he sent a band of Friars Preachers to ascertain if possible, whether they really existed, and when this was accomplished to instruct these heathen kinsfolk of his in the Christian Faith.

The friars reached the northern part of the Caucsus, and from there two of their number, Friars Julian and Bernard, pushed on, surmounting almost incredible difficulties on their journey. At last, Friar Bernard fell sick and died, so Friar Julian went on alone. Finding the way barred to him in his character of Friar Preacher, he disguised himself as the slave of a Mussulman merchant, and at last reached the land of the Bulgars on the banks of the Volga. There, in one of the villages, he met a pagan woman who spoke a dialect closely resembling that of the Magyar, and by this he knew that the tales of pagan Magyars living in Asia Minor were true. Alone he could accomplish but little in so vast a country, so he hastened back to gather another band of missionaries for the work.

On his return, however, Friar Julian found that his missionary plans could not be carried out, for in his absence storm clouds had been gathering, and all the country lay under the fear of a Tartar invasion. One of the greatest figures of his age, Genghiz Khan, had subdued Asia from the borders of China to the Indus, and from the Indian Ocean to the Caspian Sea; now his armies were threatening Eastern Europe. Andreas II was dead, bequeathing a kingdom torn by dissensions to his son Bela IV, whose Queen, Maria Lascaris, was the daughter of the fine old Greek general, Theodore, who became Emperor of Nicaea.

Friar Julian came home to find Bela struggling to uphold his royal power against the great nobles who had, little by little, made themselves almost independent in their own estates, which they dominated from fortress castles perched on rugged hill crests. When Bela heard the Friar's tale he was very glad, for he saw in this newly discovered tribe of Magyar a fresh ally, and he decided to invite them to settle in Hungary where their close personal dependence on the Crown, consequent on this invitation, would enable him to use them as a defense against the aggressions of the nobility. But this scheme, owing to the threatened Tartar invasion, came to nothing.

Every day, news of the advance of the enemy became more threatening; but the nation as a whole remained passive, for the nobles saw in it a means of extending their own power, and the common folk, on the contrary, had lived so long at peace with their neighbors, that their imaginations could not grasp the idea of battle, murder, and pillage. Even when scouts brought news that the Tartars were only five days' march from the Hungarian borders, and had exterminated the heathen Magyars, the people did not appear to recognize their peril.

But the danger was very real, and very pressing. The invaders, a hundred and twenty thousand strong, had come to a temporary halt close to the boundaries; and, what was still more serious, this was no mere marauding foray, since they had brought their women and children with them to the number of three hundred and eighty thousand. The women, as is the custom with barbarous people, saw to the putting up and taking down of the yurts[1], and performed the rest of the camp duties while the men fought. More than that, the women and children were every whit as savage as the men; and after a victory they even took their share in the ensuing carnage.

Between the Carpathian Mountains and Hungary a tribe of Cumans had settled, and there they lived at peace with their western neighbors. When they received the news of the advance of the Tartars, they were panic stricken, and forty

---

[1] Yurts are tents made of skins, and are used by the nomadic Mongols to this day.

thousand of them under their king, Kuthen, made their way to the borders of the Magyar kingdom, begging for shelter and promising to become Christians if they were permitted to enter the country. Under these conditions Bela agree, for, now that the heathen Magyars had been exterminated, he hoped that these warriors might become a support to the throne by strengthening his fighting personnel in his own struggle against his nobles. Accordingly, he and those of his counselors whom he could trust rode to the border of the realm to meet them. Bela stood sponsor to Kuthen, while those in his train became godfathers to the other pagan chieftains. Bela then gave the tribe permission to settle in the valley of the Theiss, in the eastern portion of the kingdom.

Though this plan of action seemed good to the King, the mass of the Hungarians did not at all relish this half savage addition to their ranks; for the

Cumans were violent and unruly and did not hesitate to carry out small scale raids against adjoining villages. Besides this, the Magyars read treachery, and so at last those in authority were persuaded to disperse these unwelcome visitors, suppressing the danger of having a state within a state by settling them in very small groups. Even this did not satisfy the malcontents who desired Kuthen to be driven out of the kingdom. Bela bore the brunt of this storm of indignation, and his subjects accused him of an unhealthy partiality for these strangers who were, so they declared, traitors and the advance guard of the Tartars.

In the meantime news came that these last were again on the move. In 1240 they took Kiev, the sacred city of the Russians, and in 1241 they captured Cracow. Their chief, Ogotai, a son of Genghiz Khan, had ordered his subordinate, Batou, to bring the whole basin of the Danube under subjection. Bela was fully alive to the gravity of the situation; he also knew how unprepared for battle were his subjects, so he sent his wife and three of his children to Austria, to place them under the protection of the Duke, Frederick, an ambitious princes who, earlier in the reign, had even made an attempt to seize the Hungarian throne. The two elder children were girls; Duchess Catherine, betrothed to William of Montferrat, and Duchess Margaret; the youngest, Duke Stephen, was a bay of two years old. Having done all that lay in his power for the safety of his family, Bela made the best preparations that he could to put Hungary in a state of defense by demolishing whole forests and, with the timber thus obtained, blocking the passes of the Carpathian Mountains.

Frederick left Maria Lascaris and her children in Austria, while he came himself to Hungary, ostensibly to offer assistance to Bela, but in reality to play his own game under cover of the general distraction. He supported those nobles who were disaffected to the king, and who alleged as its cause their distrust of Kuthen and his followers. The Duke's active participation in the defense of Hungary was confined to assisting the massacre of the Cumans; for while the Tartars were steadily advancing on Pesth, the Hungarian nobles turned their arms against Kuthen. Enraged at this treachery and at the murder of their king, one part of the tribe made its way out of the country spreading devastation as it went, while those who were left joined the Tartars.

On April 10th, 1241, the two armies, Bela's and Batou's, joined battle in the plain of Sajo east of the mountains of Tokay. The Magyars were utterly routed, and Bela barely escaped with his life. Three days after this battle Pesth was taken, and the women and children who had taken refuge in the

Dominican Priory were tortured with every refinement cruelty could suggest before being put to death. For a year the Tartars over-ran Hungary, since the pasturage was good and they saw no need for the moment of going further. But as they were utterly lacking in agricultural knowledge, they seized on the Magyar peasants and forced them to work as slaves. The plight of these poor people was terrible.

Bela, forced for the moment to leave the country, went first to rejoin his wife in Austria, where Frederick had already possessed himself of the gold and jewels which Maria had brought with her. Bela was taken captive by the Duke, and only released after he had paid a ransom of four thousand marks, together with the surrender of four counties. In the meantime, Maria Lascaris and her children, together with a small retinue, continued their flight southeast to the fortress of Clissa near Spalato on the Adriatic coast. Here the young

Duchess Catherine, already ill and worn down by the privations of the journey, heard that her betrothed, William of Montferrat, was dead. The news killed her, and her younger sister did not long survive her, leaving the broken-hearted Queen alone with her little son.

Bela, after paying his ransom, returned to Hungary to make an attempt at driving out the enemy. All was in vain, and in a series of rearguard actions, he was at last driven back on Spalato where his wife was already awaiting him. As he could do no more for himself, he now made appeals for help to the Pope and to Saint Louis King of France. Innocent IV had not long been crowned Pope, but already he found himself embroiled with his former friend, the Emperor Frederick II. So, from him Bela received no more than sympathy and vague promises that a Crusade should be preached against the Tartars. Saint Louis answered sadly: 'If God comes to our help we will defeat them and send them to hell; but more likely it is they who will help us to reach heaven a little sooner than we would otherwise.'

Difficulties and dangers were multiplying, for a fresh horde of barbarians, under their chief, Kadan, had crossed the Danube, captured Buda, and ravaged the country round Lake Ballaton near the Priory of Dominican nuns at Veszprim. Pushing on from there, they reached Croatia. Seeing the enemy gaining on him so swiftly, and knowing that he had now no means of beating off an attack, Bela left Spalato, and took his wife and little son to the island of Trau, a small fortress standing on a rocky, wave-fretted islet. Here he and a few immediate followers who had been left to him, prepared to make a last defense, while Kadan and his Tartars ravaged the country round.

The King was in despair; the present was dark with storm clouds and there seemed no prospect of a brighter future; his kingdom was devastated, his friends slain, his allies either powerless or unfaithful, two of his daughters were dead, and his Queen a fugitive. But Maria Lascaris, the daughter of Theodore, was made of sterner stuff and she comforted her husband with brave words of hope and trust in God. Hungary, she said, was being punished for its sins; pride, turbulence, luxury, excesses. Let them, as the sovereigns, make an offering to God of the most precious object that would ever be theirs; if their child should be a girl let her be dedicated to God and Saint Dominic from her birth; let them dedicate her now by vow as a holocaust and peace offering. Then surely, God and Saint Dominic would hear and save them and their country.

The two went outside and stood on the battlements, watching Kadan and his warriors busied in preparing rafts to ferry across to the islet. The danger was imminent, for they had no adequate defense, and within a very few hours they would, in all probability be dead, or reduced to a disgraceful slavery far worse than death. There together they offered their unborn child to God, vowing it to his service if he would save them and spare Hungary. And, even as they prayed a storm arose; wind, thunder, lightning, lashing rain, and heavy furious seas. For three days it raged with unabated fury, tearing round the island fortress, while the darkness was so profound that within the gloomy building they could not tell night from day.

Then, on the third day, as they sat in the torch-lit hall listening to the crash and rattle of the storm outside, the royal chaplain came and offered to shrive them, for the storm was beginning to abate, and now the end could not be far off. Their confessions heard, the King stood in silence awaiting the catastrophe, but the Queen knelt in prayer, repeating over and over again the words of her vow.

At last morning dawned clear, with a cloudless sky mirrored in a smooth blue sea. Mounting the battlements, the beleaguered garrison searched the farther shore for the encampments of their enemies. But there were no yurts, no columns of smoke rising in the still air, no rafts on the water or drawn up on the strand. The sea was empty, the countryside was empty. It was an undoubted miracle, or so they thought, for looking north, south, and east, nowhere could they find any traces of the Tartars. The whole host had disappeared, either drowned in the sea or blasted by lightning.

In effect, though the hand of God was certainly manifested in the happening, there was no miracle in the accepted sense of the term. It chanced that Ogotai had died far away in Asia, and this news was brought to Kadan just as the storm arose. The invasion of Europe had been all the time, in the eyes of the Tartars, more in the nature of a prolonged raid, than subjugation of the people with a view to permanent occupation. At that moment the matter of supreme importance to the barbarians on the river bank was the death of their chief, involving as it did the necessity of immediate return to Lake Baikal, where they had their headquarters, in time to share in the funeral celebrations of their old chief and the election of the new one. Faced with business of such a pressing nature to them, all thought of the Magyar King, Bela, and the final success which was already within their grasp, was wiped from their minds like writing from a slate, and with the inconsequence of children deserting an old game for a new one, the Tartars packed up their scanty belongings and left the country for ever.

They left the most appalling misery and desolation behind them, it is true. The people were starving, and there were neither crops, seed nor live stock. But difficulties only act as a spur to a brave man, and Bela returned to Buda, determined to remedy the worst of the trouble as quickly as possible. Besides he was strengthened by the knowledge that his vow had been accepted, and that within a few months the child of blessing would be born.

Chapter Three

Margaret, named after her dead sister, was from her birth a benediction to her people; for, strengthened by the knowledge of a deliverance which he could not fail to attribute to the hand of Providence and the fact that his vow had been accepted, Bela took heart again, and not only cleared out all remnants of the invaders, but ruled his country with such wisdom that in an incredibly short space of time it had regained its former prosperity. Though his policy was a short term one, results at first were all that he could desire. In order to relieve his starving people, and to enable them to cultivate the soil, he imported seed and cattle for draught purposes. He recolonized the devastated regions, partly with Magyars, partly by inviting German artisans and craftsmen into the country, and partly by persuading the Cumans who were roaming the lower Danube, to return to their old quarters in the plain of Theiss.

The King built walled cities and forts, and was specially careful to guard the eastern frontier. Hardly five years had elapsed before the country was so restored that news of another proposed invasion of the Tartars caused no dismay. Since Hungary was a country rich in minerals, it was not long before most of what the barbarians had looted had been replaced, and the nobility had once more surrounded themselves with a luxury which was almost oriental. Their bowls, cups, and plates, all were of gold or silver, and even articles in commonest use were rendered rare and beautiful by a profusion of ornament. The robes of the wealthy were of rich material magnificently embroidered. They received from Russia levies of her most valuable furs, while the east contributed rare perfumes. Their tables were spread with profusion, and their excesses in food and drink did nothing to raise the moral standard of the nobility.

For the first three years of her life the baby, Duchess Margaret, must have been clothed in the softest garments, and surrounded with every refinement of luxury. There were serving women at hand to anticipate every want, giving her all the care that love could suggest, and that her exalted rank demanded. It is necessary to bear this in mind in view of what is to follow.

From infancy this child of blessing was filled with divine grace, and with the gift of prophecy. When she was only two years old, hearing her mother talking with some anxiety about an expedition on which her father had just set out against Frederick of Austria, she said to her:

'My Lord the King will come back in safety, his army will be put to flight, but the Duke of Austria will be killed.'

And this indeed proved true in the event.

There were in Hungary at the time two convents of Dominicanesses, one at Zara, and one at Veszprim. The convent at Veszprim was noted for the regularity of its observance and the strictness of its discipline. To this convent, therefore, since their child was vowed to Saint Dominic, Margaret's parents sent her to be educated. She was only three and a half years old. With her went her foster-mother, the Countess Olympiade, widow of Count Bodomir. The Countess had seen nearly all her own children die during the Tartar invasion, and had transferred to her foster-child that love which would, in the ordinary course of events, have been theirs. Moved by this love, she herself became a nun in the Priory together with her own daughter, Sister Elizabeth, a dear friend of the little Duchess. Countess Olympiade took the habit, we are told, in order that she might serve God and look after her foster-child. In religion she was called Sister Helen, and became so famous for the holiness of her life and for the miracles that she worked that she has been beatified by the voice of the people, though her cult was never formally approved.

There were other children living in the Priory, daughters of the nobility who had been sent there to be educated, not necessarily with a view to their entering the religious life later on. This was not a boarding school in the modern sense of the word, for the young girls had to keep the enclosure as long as they lived there, and to follow a very simple manner of life. It was a peaceful and happy one, nevertheless, for the nuns considered that habits of piety were best taught and character most perfectly molded by gentle, kind, and patient treatment. Though, as a rule, such boarders are kept quite separate from the community, it does not appear that this was so at Veszprim.

It soon became obvious to the community that the baby princess who had been sent to them was no ordinary child. They knew, of course, that she had been set apart, even in her mother's womb, as belonging to God. They now saw that she had already in her fourth year attained in a great measure to the use of reason. Even before coming to the convent she had begun to serve God in earnest, and within six months of her entrance, she learned by heart the Little Office of the Blessed Virgin, and was accustomed to say it with the sisters. The Prioress gave her specially into Sister Helen's charge, desiring her to bring the little maiden up in the practice of all virtue; so Sister Helen set about teaching her Spiritual Canticles, how to recite the Office, and the behavior which befitted a virgin consecrated to God. She found Margaret an apt pupil.

One day, not long after her coming, the little one chanced to pass a Crucifix, and with childish curiosity asked what it meant. Said the nun who was with her:

'This is the Sign of the Cross on which Jesus, the Son of God, poured out his Precious Blood for us.'

And in very simple language she began to tell her the story of the Passion. Margaret with great serious eyes fixed on the narrator drank it all in just as every child is wont to be enthralled by stories of our Lord. But this little girl of four years understood far more than any ordinary child, for her mind stretched far beyond the love story as a mere history. In some way she gathered what was behind it, what it meant to her, and the return of love she was constrained to make. She stretched out her arms and hugged the Crucifix, covering it with tears and kisses. Then she cried aloud:

'Lord'—for so she had heard the courtiers address her father—'Me too.' And falling on her knees, she made the *venia* as she had seen the nuns do when they lay prostrate to ask pardon for a fault committed. Stretching out her little arms in the form of the Cross which hung above her, she showed her Jesus as well as she was able that she meant to join him there.

The God of children had wooed and won his little spouse. From that day until her death, the Cross spoke to her of all the Mysteries of Faith. She never passed one without falling prostrate in adoration before it; and her greatest treasure was a small wooden Crucifix in which was a fragment taken from the wood of the true Cross. Before dinner and supper she always paid a visit to the great Rood in the Chapter Room, and often she so lost herself that after 'second tables' when the second serving of the meal was finished they had to fetch her to her food.

The other children were very fond of Margaret—probably she was the youngest of them—and liked her to join in their games. Now, play means something very different to children from what it does to grown people. A child's play is a far more serious matter to it than many a grown person's most important duties are to them. Children carry out their impersonations with the greatest earnestness, and if one hears them laugh it is never about the game as a game, but because of some defect in the impersonation which strikes them as ludicrous. When the other little girls asked Margaret to play:

'Let us go to Church,' she would answer, 'and talk to our Lord and our Lady. That is the best play that I know.' They would go with her, of course; no one ever refused that child anything, and it is surely not straining credulity too far to suggest that those whom they visited made it in every way 'the best play', knowing so completely what would please and interest their guests. At other times when the children coaxed her to go with them to play, she would say:

'Let us first go to the Church and say a "Hail Mary" to our Lady and then we will go and play.'

On Fridays she would join neither in games nor conversation; for she simply could not understand how people, having once heard of the Crucifixion could ever place it anywhere but as the centre and dominating influence of their whole lives. And as love begets love and the desire of likeness to the Beloved, so there grew up in the heart of this little child an ever increasing thirst for penance. Her one desire was to suffer by way of expiation and in order to prove her love.

When she was still only four years old she asked for the Dominican Habit; and when her wish was granted, she received it at her Clothing with such gravity and reverence that everyone was struck by the strength of purpose shown in so young a child. Prayer was the breath of her life, and it was almost impossible to curtail her devotions. If her Mistress, the Venerable Helen, tried to cut short her prayers, fearing for her health, she cried so bitterly that the nun, apprehensive lest her grief should prove even more injurious to her health than her prayers, was obliged to yield and let her go her own way.

Margaret clung to Helen, calling her Mother, and trying to imitate her in all things. When she was five years old, her Mistress, having in remembrance the Magyar tendency to luxury and self-indulgence which might well be strengthened by the fact that the little Duchess was of the Blood Royal, and realizing as well that her charge was no ordinary child, made her a tiny hair-shirt or girdle, meaning her to learn its use by wearing it occasionally. She did this, as the Life tells us, not because she had no pity for the child, but that the saintly little maid might become accustomed to the use of such things, which are worn by very many servants of God to tame the flesh.

Margaret took the girdle and put it on at once. But the episode ended in a way that Helen certainly had never foreseen when she gave it to the child. Having once put it on, her charge showed no intention of ever taking it off again, but wore it every day. This would not do at all, so Helen confiscated it altogether, telling the child that she was far too young for such practices. So Margaret was obliged to wait with considerable impatience until she should be considered old enough, which was when she had reached her seventh year.

From this time on there was constant friendly warfare between the little Duchess and her foster-mother, for while Helen was perpetually striving to mitigate the child's austerities, Margaret was clinging to them just as tenaciously. All through her life this combat continued. When her Superiors remonstrated with her, she wept and pleaded so piteously that they were unwillingly obliged to let her go her own way. And the God who inspired her thirst for penance saw to it that those in authority were literally unable to impose obedience on her in this matter. It goes without saying that she would have submitted at once to a command or even a definitely expressed wish, but our Lord never let it come to that, though she must have suffered an added pain in knowing that her Superiors were troubled and perplexed. But in spite of their anxiety, Margaret's Prioresses must have been comforted to know that her Confessor, a saintly and prudent Dominican, knew and approved of all that she did; it relieved them of responsibility in the matter.

We do not know when Margaret made her First Communion, but this we do know, that after receiving the Blessed Sacrament, she was often raised a foot or more into the air. From the Elevation of the Sacred Host to the Communion of the Mass she was frequently in ecstasy; and her love of the Holy Name of Jesus was so great that, like Saint Bernard, she found no other name so sweet in her ears. This was when she was still a child of only six or seven years old.

After some years, Margaret's father, desiring to have his daughter near him, decided to build a convent for her on an island in the Danube not far from Buda. This islet had originally been named the Isle of Hares, but after the Priory had been built there it was renamed Saint Mary of the Isle. Now it is known as Margareten Insel, though the convent there has long since fallen into decay.

As soon as the building was finished, the King petitioned the Master General of the Dominican Order, John the Teutonic, to accept it for his nuns, and to bring there from Veszprim his daughter, Margaret, with as many other nuns as should be fitting. Master John the Teutonic was a close personal friend of both Bela and his Queen, even though it was he who had once been entrusted with the delicate task of excommunicating Andreas the King's father. For this very reason Bela was probably glad of this chance of showing his own loyalty to the Order.

The Master General accepted the gift, and established in the newly-built convent a small community of nuns from Veszprim, Margaret among them. The Prioress was Sister Catherine who had been her first teacher of Latin. The others were Sisters Eliana, Agatha, Alexandrine, Benedict, Cecilia, and Helena; most of whom will be met with again in the course of the narrative. Sister Elizabeth, Margaret's foster-sister, accompanied her mother, as did Sister Judith, another of Margaret's young companions, who used to discuss with her what they read, and who learnt many prayers with her. Before the death of the Saint, the community numbered over seventy.

Margaret herself was just ten years old at the time, a very earnest mature novice in her white habit and veil, with a soul as white as the habit, and all her energy concentrated on living the kind of life that she knew would be pleasing to her beloved. She was most determined that her worldly rank should be forgotten, and was anxious to receive none of the respect and privileges which might be offered to a Religious of the Blood Royal, but simply to be regarded as plain Sister Margaret a novice. It was difficult and wearisome at times to make others remember this and to prevent them showing her the respect due to her worldly rank. Sometimes she grew so tired of this that she would say:

'I know of only one thing in the world which makes me sad, and that is that I was born in a castle instead of a thatched hut in some far away village. Then I should only be worth what I am in myself, and not what I owe to my parents.'

The King and Queen, as was natural, came to see their daughter as often as they were permitted, and that was more often than Margaret desired. If she happened to be in Choir when they were announced, she would never go to them until the Hour of Office was ended; for an earthly King must give precedence to a Heavenly One.

As a matter of course, the visitors brought with them presents calculated to please any ordinary girl; pieces of embroidered cloth, jewels, and such things. In those days parents very often provided their daughters' clothes, and these in Margaret's case were certainly the best obtainable. She received the gifts with courtesy, and then gave the whole away, with the leave of her Prioress, either through her or through her Confessor, the Dominican Provincial Father Marcellus, to be sold for the poor or given to churches. Then by way of compensating herself for the vexation of being treated like a royal princess she used to beg from the Habit Mistress a habit to wear which was a little older and coarser than those worn by the rest of the community.

Since she was so determined that every part of her being should give its quota to the honor and service of her Spouse, she was not content with offering the love of her heart, but trained mind and memory until she could repeat the entire Psalter by heart, as well as many other portions of the Divine Office. And because she was a true daughter of her Holy Father Saint Dominic, she also committed to memory the Latin version of the Conference of Cassian which are read in the Refectory during the collation; and for which Saint Dominic had so much veneration.

Chapter Four

On the Feast of All Saints, 1252, the Dominican Master General died. Before his death he had promised Bela and his wife, to whose devoted friendship he could refuse nothing, that the General Chapter of 1253 should be held for the first time at Buda. Owing to his death no General Chapter was held in 1253, but on May 31st, 1254, the Capitular Fathers assembled according to promise at Buda, where they received a princely welcome, in order to elect a new Master General. Humbert de Romans, one of the most famous men who have ever governed the Order, was unanimously elected Master General.

The Priory of Saint Mary of the Isle was all but finished; the King and Queen had defrayed the whole cost of building, had endowed it with royal munificence, and now they asked Blessed Humbert to take formal possession of it in the name of the Order. They desired also that at the same time he should receive the Solemn Vows of their daughter Margaret, now twelve years old, and according to the custom of the time of an age to make them. The Master General came willingly, and Margaret made her Vows at his hands. Both her father and mother were present, and in honor of the occasion gave further handsome gifts to the Priory.

Although Sister Margaret desired nothing but to be permitted to remain a poor unknown religious, she could not help being likewise the daughter of the King of Hungary, and more important even than this, the fame of her virtues had already spread far and wide. Many people of all ranks and classes came from all over the country to get a sight of her if they could, and commend themselves to her prayers. When obedience sent her to the parlor, she showed herself gracious to everyone, but her guests were also conscious of a certain aloofness; she was possessed of a dignity and repose of manner which is usually only found coupled with maturity; the expression of her face was always calm and serene, and no one ever saw depicted on it either dejection or excessive elation.

Hence, in spite of herself, she was something of a personage even beyond the confines of her own country, and was, moreover, of considerable political importance. When she was still very young, a Duke of Poland, probably Boleslaus the Pious who later married her sister Iolanthe, asked for her hand in marriage. Her sister

Saint Cunegunde was already the wife of Boleslaus the Chaste, and with her husband was following in the footsteps of Saint Henry the Emperor and the earlier Saint Cundegunde. But the second offer, and that the most difficult to refuse, was made by Ottokar, King of Bohemia.

The Iron King, as he was called, was a man of boundless ambition and during his reign he conquered Austria, Styria, Carinthia, and Carniola, extending his Kingdom to the shores of the Adriatic. During the earlier part of his reign he had been at war with Bela; but later on he changed his tactics, and determined to seek an alliance with Hungary. Accordingly, in 1260, he made a treaty of peace with Bela. The peace conference was held on Saint Mary's Isle, and at the conclusion of the business, Ottokar asked to be allowed to visit Lady Margaret of whose sanctity he had heard so much.

Bela found it difficult not to accede to the request, so he took the Bohemian King to the Priory.

Margaret was eighteen years old at the time, and, as we are told, exceedingly beautiful in face and person; her loveliness being still further enhanced by its unadorned simplicity, and the truth and purity of her soul which shone in her face. Reasons of statecraft had no weight in the choice of Ottokar of Bohemia, for he at once fell deeply in love with the maiden herself. Without more ado, he made his proposal to Bela; if the Hungarian King would give him his daughter in marriage, he, Ottokar, promised that there should be perpetual alliance between Hungary and Bohemia. There need be no question of dowry, for he would not accept one; in lieu thereof he would endow his bride elect with the whole of his own kingdom.

As the memory of his salvation from the Tartar menace faded from Bela's mind, so apparently did the memory of his own vow, for he began to consider the question of Ottokar's marriage to his daughter quite seriously. After some thought and consultation he answered:

'Such a thing, my Lord King, is not easy, since the young Duchess has been vowed to God from her infancy, and, moreover, when she realized what we had done, on reaching the years of discretion, she herself has ratified this engagement by making her Profession as a Dominican at the hands of no less a person than the Master General himself.'

Ottokar, nothing daunted, offered to send to Rome himself for the required dispensation, and by degrees so worked on his host that Bela agreed to the marriage under conditions.

'If, when the dispensation comes, my daughter Margaret will agree to the marriage, then I shall be very happy to give my consent.' And with this Ottokar was well content, for he could not conceive any maiden of her own free will refusing so good a marriage.

In due time the dispensation did arrive, and now it only remained for Bela to fulfill his share of the bargain and obtain his daughter's consent. By this time both King and Queen had so thoroughly succeeded in convincing themselves that they were acting for the best in view of all the good that was bound to accrue from the marriage that they approached Margaret and gave her in all good faith what they considered the best of reasons to induce her to take the step. She had dedicated herself to God on behalf of Hungary, in fulfillment of a vow, it was true, but in accepting this offer she was still sacrificing herself for her country though in another way. The Pope had been asked to annul her Vows and he had done so, in fact they had brought the dispensation with them; she could hardly refuse a course of action of which Rome approved.

Margaret was shocked and horrified, though perhaps hardly taken altogether by surprise, for she had heard talk of this kind before. She listened in silence until her parents had finished and then she said:

'I beg of you, my father, never again to ask me to consent to an earthly marriage. You know that when I was a baby you espoused me to Jesus Christ. Now have you so far forgotten your promise made to God; have you so completely changed your mind, that you now command me to forsake my Heavenly Spouse, to violate the integrity of my body and soul, to marry a mere sinful man? I will never give up the life to which I am vowed; always will I remain a maid, for never will I soil the purity, the virginity of my body and soul, that virginity which I have already dedicated to the King of kings.

'I remember how, when I was but seven years old, you tried to espouse me to the Polish Duke. And I think you will remember, likewise, the answer that I gave you then. I told you that while I lived I wished to serve him only to whom you had espoused me at my birth. If then, when I was but a child, I would in no wise yield to your will in opposition to the claims of truth and justice, do you think that I am likely to give in to you, now that I am older and wiser, and am, in consequence, more capable of grasping the greatness of the Divine Grace that has been vouchsafed to me? Cease, then, my Father, from trying to turn me from my determination to remain a Religious. For, since I prefer the Heavenly Kingdom to that which has been offered me by the King of Bohemia, so also do I prefer to die rather than obey these your commands which will bring death to my soul.'

She ceased to speak and sat watching her parents, but they for a moment or two could find nothing to answer. Then Bela plucked up courage, determined not to give in without a battle, and began once again to recapitulate the reasons which made this marriage desirable from the point of view of the Magyar people, the only spot on which he had any hope of Margaret proving vulnerable. He pointed out also that, as she was at one and the same time his daughter and his subject, she was bound to obey him both as her father and her King. He ended:

'Are we not your parents? And does not the Gospel command you to reverence and obey your parents?'

Margaret stopped him, saying: 'As often as you command what is pleasing to God I will obey you as my parent and as my master; but if you command me to do what is contrary to God's Will, then you are neither my parent nor my master, and I will never obey you as such. I would rather cut off my nose and my lips than consent to such a thing. And, mark my words, if matters ever come to such a pass and I am driven to it, I will surely put an end to the whole affair by mutilating myself, so that I shall never again be desirable to any man.'

She had won the first round of the combat, and the King of Bohemia was dismissed, foiled for the moment but not definitely defeated. He returned home, and from his own Capital sent an embassy, again requesting Margaret's hand in marriage. Humanly speaking, this placed the King in a very awkward position, for to offend so powerful a monarch at such a juncture was a serious matter. The King appears to have decided to abide by his daughter's decision without more question; for it is the Queen this time who takes up the matter. She sent for Father Marcellus, the Dominican Provincial, and explained the case to him.

'Father, for very grave reasons the King has decided that our daughter is to be married to the King of Bohemia. We have already obtained a Papal dispensation of her Vows. Go to her, then, signify to her the wishes of her parents, and try to discover her own feeling on the matter.'

The Provincial agreed to go into the question with Margaret; accordingly, he made his way to Saint Mary of the Isle. There he asked to see Sister Margaret, and as the object of his visit was an important matter, he also asked that the Prioress and Sister Helen Olympiade should be present as witnesses. Before these two he interrogated Margaret concerning her proposed marriage. She answered at once and without the slightest hesitation:

'You may take this for a certainty, Father, that I prefer to die a thousand times rather than obey my parents in this matter. I have made my Profession here of my own free will; I am here because God, in my firm belief, wishes me to be here. No persuasions, and no violence will be of any avail to make me renounce my vocation.'

The battle was finally won and the King of Bohemia was told that there was absolutely no hope of Margaret's changing her mind. But, since statecraft, as well as love, was playing a part in the proposed marriage, he agreed to espouse, in her stead, Duchess Cunegunde the Younger, Margaret's niece, the daughter of her sister, Duchess Anne. Later, Ottokar saw fit to change his policy of friendship with Hungary and became instead her most implacable enemy.

That Margaret was ready to suffer anything rather than sacrifice her chastity received further confirmation from a remark that she made to a group of sisters about that time. Sister Margaret, daughter of Duke William of Makonie, was among those who heard her, and who afterwards gave witness at the Process of Beatification. They were speaking of rumors which were current that the Tartars were preparing a large army for a fresh invasion of Hungary; and one of the nuns remarked that it was the custom of those barbarians to violate virgins. Said Margaret, for once proud and regal:

'I know what I would do in that case. I would slit by lips and cut off my nose; and then, when the Tartars saw how unsightly I was, they would leave me alone.'

We may be sure that this was no mere empty talk.

In order to put an end, once and for all, to any further matrimonial projects on the part of her father, Margaret determined to seek the consecration of her virginity to God by the ancient sacramental rite that was already rare in the Church and was not used in her Order. The solemn ceremony follows step by step that of an Ordination. It is reserved to the bishop and can never be repeated. She applied to her good friend the Provincial, Father Marcellus, and he arranged the matter with the Archbishop. In her case it was judged expedient in order to make Margaret perfectly secure from further persecution.

Accordingly, at the age of eighteen or nineteen she was solemnly Consecrated before the Altar of her aunt, Saint Elizabeth of Hungary, by Benedict Archbishop of Esztergom, to whom belonged the privilege of administering the Sacraments to the Royal Family, though this ceremony was of course no Sacrament. There were three other religious, also of the Blood Royal, who were consecrated at the same time.

The ceremony includes the blessing of the veil, the ring, and the crown. In Margaret's case, following the customs of the Hungarians at a royal wedding, this crown was of gold, and after its benediction it was placed on her head by the Count Palatine. She lifted it off, and taking it in her hands, she crossed the Church to lay it at the foot of the great Rood; a symbol that henceforth she belonged to none but her Crucified Master.

But even this solemn Consecration did not finally end the persecution that Margaret suffered at the hands of her father.

Charles of Anjou, brother of Saint Louis of France, but unlike him in every respect, was made King of Naples in the year 1266. It occurred to Bela that he might ensure the peace of his own kingdom by uniting the Royal houses of Arpad and Anjou. His thought turned again to Margaret, and he proposed marrying her to Charles, assuring the latter that he could easily obtain a dispensation from her Vows from the Pope Clement IV. Margaret's answer was always the same. She desired only to preserve her virginity for the Lord Jesus Christ. And according to the Decretal Letter of her Canonization, 'the Divine Spouse, always faithful and ever more generous, set up in the heart of his handmaid a sweet dwelling place, adorned it most lavishly with heavenly gifts, and made her an associate of his Passion, and a partaker of his consolation and power during life and after death as well.'

But our Lord likewise promised to those who leave father and mother for his sake the hundredfold in this life *with* persecutions. By this last refusal to comply with his will, Margaret drew down on herself the wrath of her father. In order to bend her to his wishes, he first attempted to cajole her by flattery, and when she fearlessly rebuked him for again attempting to turn her from her holy purpose, his anger was roused and the Saint had to endure much persecution at his hands. But, entirely fearless, Margaret stood her ground, and endured all dauntlessly.

The remainder of her short life was buried in Christ, nailed with him to the Cross, passed in the practice of the most heroic mortification. Being in all things a true daughter of Saint Dominic, she sought freedom of spirit in the practice of rugged penance; thus, satisfying at one and the same time her devotion to Christ Crucified, and the apostolic spirit which burned in her. In addition, she accepted in its fullest spirit the role of victim for the sins of her people. Therefore, to the penances of her burning love, she added others of a peculiar type which can only be understood in this light. For it appears to have been borne in on her that, in order to carry out her role of victim, it was incumbent on her to practice in a marked degree the virtues in which, as a nation, the Magyars were deficient.

Chapter Five

Love is a passion which has one single source in the soul, it may differ in its object, it is true; often, indeed, its object is wrongly named, for what is termed love of another is in reality merely love of self. It may differ also in its manifestations; for it is sometimes passive, desiring only to rest in the presence of the Beloved. At other times it is an active force, seeking to spend itself in service of the loved one. But, whatever may be its end, whatever its form of manifestation, the power in itself remains one single thing, a reaching out to union with the object beloved. It follows then that the love given to God is the same that we give to our fellow men, and manifests itself in the same ways; Mary at the Master's Feet, Martha busied with much serving. In this respect, the chief difference between the saints and ourselves is that their love is an all pervading power, not merely a matter of duty having one anchor in love of self; the love of the saints reaches out to God and to the all-pure, all-perfect Human Nature of God the Son with an intensity which we ordinary folk cannot fathom.

This is the true, indeed it is the only possible, explanation of all their self-inflicted sufferings. Love begets a burning desire of union, which means no other than transformation into the likeness of the Beloved. A saint, for instance, cannot face a Crucifix unless he also bears on his body the marks of Christ's sufferings; he cannot remain a delicately nurtured member under a thorn-crowned

Head. So it is only in living lives filled with penance such as we find baffling or even revolting, that the saints discover happiness, which is, after all, the goal for each one of us, and without which life would be impossible. It seems that in their intensity of desire for likeness with Christ Crucified we can find an explanation of how they contrive to gain the consent of confessors, and superiors to a manner of life which would never be tolerated in other people.

In studying the lives of the saints, there is also another factor to be borne in mind; we only know what others tell us about the majority of them, the triumphant side of their self-crucifixion. But if these servants of God are to be of any practical help to us on our road to heaven, it is necessary to remember that it is human agony, human disgust, shrinking, and weariness which they carry upwards on the broad wings of their love.

Margaret was such a lover, and because her life had been pure and unspotted from babyhood, her love of God and of his only-begotten Son, Jesus Christ our Lord, burned with a white heat of intensity which of necessity carried in its train a tormenting thirst for suffering which was well-nigh unendurable. She was irresistibly driven to copy him.

Her Lord had been poor and a laborer from his youth, and so she likewise was in love with poverty. Her garments were always coarser and rougher than those of her sisters; and this at a time when Royalty, even in the cloister, received as its right special privileges and Margaret's rank would thereby have entitled her to clothes of a better quality.

Margaret's habit was always torn and patched, nor would she change it for another unless that were patched likewise. If her cappa, the black cloak of the Dominican habit, fell to pieces she would beg two old ones and by piecing the better strips, made one wearable cappa for herself. And we may be sure that the 'Benedictus Deus' and the profound inclination with which she received the poor rags that she coaxed from the Habit Mistress, was no perfunctory matter of routine.

Her veil was heavy and coarse, and if, by chance, she received a better one, she would exchange it with whomsoever she could persuade to do her this favor. If her parents brought her new clothes and she was obliged to put them on, she hurried off to scour pots and pans, sweep floors, and do other dirty work until all signs of newness had worn off; nor would she relinquish her habit until it was dropping to pieces with age. Then, when she was conspicuous only by her shabbiness she rejoiced.

To her patched, shabby garments she added a hair shirt, which she wore every week from Thursday until Compline on Saturday, on the Vigils and Ember Days, and throughout the whole of Lent and Advent. When she was twelve years old, Father Marcellus, her Confessor, himself a great servant of God, understanding the thirst for suffering which consumed her, gave her a belt of horsehair, knotted with boars' bristles the whole made into a kind of net knotted at every join. Lest others should see this, she sewed in old sleeves reaching from the elbow to the wrist, under this she wore an iron girdle drawn tight into the flesh.

At night she changed this garment for a belt made of hedgehog skins, three of four fingers in width, with the spines turned inward. Only two persons knew of the 'garment of her delights', the Prioress and Sister Alexandrine who had charge of the hedgehogs. The skins were cured and sewn by one of the serving maids who worked outside the enclosure, but she would not have known their purpose. Two years after her death, this girdle was shown to the assembled Friars of the Order by the Master General, John of Vercelli, when the General Chapter was held at Pesth in 1273.

Her arms she often bound with ropes made of dogskin, and she fastened sharp pointed nails upwards on the inside of her sandals. Once, when she had been meditating on the barbarous fashion in which our Lord's hands had been tied, her agony was so great that she begged Sister Anne to tie her own hands tightly together with a strong piece of rope. Poor Sister Anne could not escape her importunities, and in her own trouble of mind, tied the Saint's hands so tightly that she nearly broke the bones.

Our Lord was scourged too, and there was only one way in which she was able to bear the thought of this scourging; every night she disciplined herself to blood, often with rods, or bunches of twigs, or strips of hedgehog skin. Often she forced the nuns whom she most trusted in the community to do her this greatest favor. They dreaded to be asked for she never rested until the blood flowed, so they shrank from the ordeal and kept out of the way when they could. Margaret, however, was a princess accustomed to the absolute right of command which was the birthright of great folk in those days, but which was only invoked by her on occasions such as these; then those she commanded did not dare to refuse. The Dormitory was too public, so she took the chosen sister to a secret spot of her own. There she saw to it that she was given no respite until the other, weeping bitterly, was wearied out.

One day, when she was receiving the discipline in this way from her foster-sister, Sister Elizabeth, she kept saying to her:

'Strike hard, do not be afraid, have no mercy.'

Sister Sabina said that she often gave her the discipline; and Sister Benedict deposed that she gave her the discipline at times until she was ready to drop with fatigue and emotion. On the last three days of Holy Week, she took or received this penance every hour.

It happened one night that she took a certain nun, Sister Sabina, with her to a secret place for this purpose. No sooner had she bared her shoulders than a bright light shown through the whole room. It covered Sister Margaret as with a robe of radiant beauty, remaining thus until she had again dragged the habit over her torn bleeding shoulders, then it vanished to be replaced by an exquisite fragrance, which lingered in the place for a considerable time. Two sisters happened to be passing, and they noticed the bright light which shone from the room. Anxious lest a fire should have broken out, they opened the door to find Margaret standing bathed in this heavenly glow. Falling on their knees the begged her to remember them in her prayers.

It was only by practicing penances such as these that Margaret found it possible to go to her favorite place of prayer before a Crucifix. Those outstretched arms drew her so that she could not stay away, and yet she was only permitted by her love to kneel there when she too was wounded and scarred. Then, as she lay prostrate at the foot of the Cross, she could repeat in all sincerity and truth the prayer she had first made when she was only four years old: 'Me too.'

The Dominican Dormitory in those days consisted of a long corridor down either wall of which stood the cells, small cubicles open to the passage in front, but separated one from the other by partitions five or six feet high, so that, while each one was a separate compartment, all were open to those who passed down the dormitory passage. Night after Night Margaret kept tryst there with her Divine Spouse on the mountain slopes of Palestine. From nightfall until the hour of Matins she watched and prayed, and often from the end of Matins until daybreak. So that no one should know of this, she used to lie down as soon as the bell for Matins rang, so that she might appear to rise with the others. Afterwards she would disturb her bed covering so that the bed might look as if it had been used. There were times, however, when the brave spirit was no longer able to drive the worn body, and then the nun who called her used to find Margaret asleep lying on the floor beside the bed.

Our Lord had fasted, and so Margaret fasted too. On account of her rank, and her delicate upbringing, she could, according to the idea of the time, have claimed slightly better fare than the rest; in fact, provided that the quality of the food was adhered to, and no meat or other fare forbidden by the Constitutions was sent, there was no reason why she should not have received portions from the royal table; but she would have none of it. If her portion was not identical with that served to the others she grew angry. She asked only one privileged, and that was to lose all claim to preference; why would not her sisters accord her this one request? When her family came to visit her she was expected according to the then custom to take her meal with them in the parlor; but this she would never do if she could help it, preferring to share the common meal with her sisters in the Refectory.

Often enough as she sat at table with the rest of the community, she would let all food pass her untasted, while she sat, her hand shading her eyes, lost in God. When she did eat, she ate sparingly, and as soon as her meal was finished, following custom, she dropped her veil over her face to gaze uninterrupted on him whom her soul loved.

From the Feast of the Exaltation of the Holy Cross until Easter she carried out the Rule of the Order to the letter and fasted most rigorously. Sometimes it happened that the Prioress wished to dispense her, for she was not strong and she worked hard. She would send for Margaret to tell her she was not to fast for a time. On such occasions Margaret said nothing, she just stood in silence and wept and wept, until the Prioress, conquered by her tears, and enlightened by the spirit which we call 'grace of office,' left her free to fast as it pleased her.

On the Vigils of Christmas, Pentecost, and the Nativity of our Lady and the vigils of many other saints, and on all Wednesdays and Fridays, she fasted on bread and water. Then, and only then, did she obtain permission to do what she would have been obliged to do if she had been dispensed from the fasts of the Order; she took her meals apart so that no one should know what she was doing. She hated to appear singular in anything.

Never, during the whole of her religious life, did she touch meat. Abstinence from meat is enjoined by Saint Dominic in the Constitutions of his Order; but he allows also for the wise privilege of dispensation, and the sick in the Infirmary, and those in weak health are given meat, but not in the common Refectory. There was only one thing for Margaret to do if she wished to avoid eating meat.

Ill or well she must never have her meals in the Infirmary, where she would be obliged under obedience to eat what the Infirmarian gave her. And so, all her life long she kept silence on the subject of her illnesses, for had she acknowledged sickness, the care of her health would have devolved entirely on the Infirmarian. Once, when she was seriously ill for six weeks on end, she said nothing about it, but went on with her prayers and work as usual; somehow she kept on her feet that nothing might interfere with the practice of the penance which was the breath of life to her.

From the age of four years she had always fasted on Good Friday. As she grew older, during the last three days of Holy Week, she neither ate nor slept. During the whole of that time, except when she was saying Office with the community or on her knees in private prayer, she was either standing erect, or stretched prostrate before the Altar of the

Holy Cross. Only when the Vespers of Holy Saturday were sung, would she go into one of the oratories and there allow herself a little sleep.

Chapter Six

Saint Margaret had yet another task before her; she had been offered as a victim for the salvation of Hungary even before her birth, and as soon as she could understand what this meant she herself confirmed it wholeheartedly. Before her there had been no nun of the Blood Royal in Hungary, and she, its first fruit, was to offer herself as a holocaust of expiation. As soon, therefore, as she had made herself secure from all possibility of worldly entanglement by taking her Vows, and by her further solemn Consecration, she prepared herself to carry out to its utmost extent the role she had accepted with such a willing heart. The austere life of penance that she was already leading seemed to her as nothing, and in any case she was constrained to this by her passionate love of our Lord. What more was there that she could do?

Hungary was at that time a land of contrasts; the nobles as a class were possessed by a passion for independence and a love of luxury. Nowhere in Europe were the clothes of richer material or more elaborately adorned, nowhere was to be found more valuable or elaborate house furnishings, as the Magyar nobility set themselves to carry out their somewhat barbaric ideal of grandeur in profusion. In disposition, too, they were quarrelsome with their equals, harsh and oppressive towards their inferiors; they were turbulent also, being moved by a jealous pride and susceptibility, which rendered them impatient of all authority. For these Margaret was a victim of expiation.

At the very doors of the castles of these proud and luxury loving lords, stood the hovels of their wretched serfs, dirty, poor, hungry, degraded, slaves in all but name. So unsavory were the persons and homes of these poor peasants that their own masters avoided close contact with them. For these, too, Margaret was a victim of expiation.

She understood what she had taken on herself; she knew that she must redouble her merciless usage of her body, her ruthless spoliation of self-will and self-gratification, her detachment from all goods of this world. With the relentless logic of faith and generosity, she set herself to carry out her purpose daily until death. Somehow, and in some way, she must make herself lower and more abject than the meanest beggar in her father's kingdom; she must find a way to place herself beneath the feet of all. Whether all this was explicitly in her mind, or whether she only understood it in general terms we have no means of knowing; the result seems to point to explicit realization; but, in any case, this aspect of her spiritual life seems capable of no other explanation than that love and clear sighted truth showed her the way to carry out her role of victim in every detail.

In the first place she ceased to regard the cleanliness of her own person and clothing. The rest of the community did not relish this at all. They remonstrated with her. They told her to take more care of her personal cleanliness, and to change her habit more frequently. When she turned a deaf ear to their remonstrances and quietly pursued her own course, many of them began to avoid her. She watched them, and when she saw on many of their faces the same look of half suppressed disgust that she had seen on those of the folk outside when they came in too close contact with the beggars she was content, for she had found a way to place herself under the feet of all.

One day she remarked a little drily to a sister who was complaining that her services to the poor and utter disregard of personal cleanliness were making her verminous:

'Dear Sister, permit me to be tormented in this way for the love of our Lord Jesus Christ. You need have no fear of yourself on this score, I can assure you, I shall keep them for myself alone.'

In this connection a very beautiful story is told. There was a certain Friar of great repute among the Franciscans. One day he related in the presence of witnesses among whom were several Dominicans, that he had had a dream in which he had seen Sister Margaret standing before him; to his astonishment, he saw that the lice on her habit were all changed to jewels of dazzling whiteness and purity, which embroidered the edge of both her habit and scapular.

She would have nothing to do with baths, nor with the unguents and salves which were their equivalent. Occasionally she would permit another sister to bathe her feet, but excepting for that, whatever services were needed, she performed for herself. Sick or well, she never wore linen and she slept in her clothes.

In order to carry the principle of substitution still further, she constituted herself the servant of the community. With her besom of twigs bound to a wooden handle, she swept the church, the cloisters, the dormitory, and the Refectory. Then she went to the kitchen and scoured the pots and pans. She made a regular practice of cleaning the fish for the midday meal. In summer this was merely a disagreeable, dirty piece of work; but in winter it was far worse, for the sharp scales of the fish, and the cold water in which she washed them, made her hands raw and bleeding. But that troubled her not a whit.

Often she served the midday meal in the Refectory. This consisted of two cooked dishes, usually a vegetable soup and fish; eggs and milk foods were allowed when it was not a fasting season. Margaret used to carry round the first portion, and, while the sisters were eating it, she slipped away to pray before the Crucifix in the Church or Chapter Room, returning in time to carry round the second dish. Then, the meal ended, often enough she would slip away without breaking her fast.

She had a special charity towards the sick, and was never so happy as when she was looking after them, for she served them with the greatest devotion. When there was a kindness to be done, she possessed very sharp eyes and so she was generally the first to notice when a member of the community was ailing, and as soon as she became aware of the fact, she went at once to the Prioress to petition for leave to look after the sick sister. It appears that, for part at least of her religious life, she was one of the Infirmarians; for in this connection a story is told.

The Provincial came on one of his periodic visits to the Priory at Saint Mary of the Isle, and on this occasion he arrived accompanied by some other friars. As there were several nuns sick at the time, he and his companions went into the enclosure to visit and console them. The Prioress, Sister Margaret and some of the other nuns accompanied the party. Among the sick were four young novices who were seriously ill and in high fever. After the Provincial had talked to them for a few moments, one of them suggested that if he were really sorry for them, he would command Sister Margaret to pray for them. Accordingly, he turned to the Saint:

'What is this, Sister Margaret?' he cried in mock rebuke, 'How is it that you leave your young sisters to suffer so? Where is your pity? Now, hurry off at once and pray for them perseveringly that their Lord will have mercy on them and restore them to health.'

Margaret smiled deprecatingly and sweetly as was her wont, but said nothing. Later on, as soon as the Provincial and his companions had gone, she went to the little Oratory, as she had been told, to carry out the obedience imposed on her. The next morning, when those in charge of the four novices went to visit them, they found all of them in perfect health and entirely free from any trace of fever.

As the community at Saint Mary of the Isle was a very large one, there were naturally a number of sick, and Sister Margaret was in her element looking after them. The number never troubled her. She would go from one to the other, making their beds, sweeping the Infirmary, and preparing baths for them. This involved drawing water from the well and carrying it upstairs. Then she fetched billets from the wood shed, which she carried up on her own shoulders, lit the fires and heated water. Then there was soiled linen to wash, and this she did, summer and winter alike, standing in the water of the river and rubbing the dirty clothes between two stones as the manner was.

There were, of course, no butchers to clean and joint the meat, so she used to carry large portions up to the Infirmary on her shoulders and prepare them herself. Once when she was very busy turning a joint of meat on the spit, another nun came into the room and, seeing how hot and tired Margaret was looking, said to her:

'Hand that over to me, Sister, and let me take a turn.' Margaret looked up, shaking her head with an amused little smile:

'No! No! Dearest Sister. That will not do at all, for if I hand over this work to you, you would acquire the merit of humility for yourself and deprive me of it.'

And she went on with her labor of love.

But the sick of the community did not suffice for her charity. They, after all, were the Spouses of Christ Jesus, and it was an honor to serve them. In those days, serving maids were employed in convents; they took no Vows, but were apparently bound to enclosure, and lived within the precincts of the place; these, when sick, Margaret took under her care. They were, many of them, but ill-acquainted with the common decencies of life, and this was Sister Margaret's golden opportunity when she constituted herself their servant. She washed them, tended them, cleaned out their quarters. Nothing daunted her, nor did she show the slightest sign of disgust, however objectionable the service she was rendering them might be.

For instance, some of them, especially the children of the laborers employed on the farm, were in a sorry condition of dirt and sores. But Margaret took the cleaning of verminous heads, and of body sores which generally resulted from filth and neglect, quite as a matter of course, and persevered until the cure was complete; though she must have known that in many cases it was merely labor lost. So conscientious was she in her self-imposed task that she had been known to doctor dirty heads no fewer than seven times in one day.

In the Infirmary was a certain Sister Elizabeth, a very large, obese woman and a complete invalid, probably paralyzed, for she had lain unable to do anything for herself for eighteen years. She was so mountainous, and so helpless, that several sisters had already sacrificed their own health in looking after her; and it appears that at the last the community had given up the attempt to do more than feed her; for hygiene, as we know it, is a comparatively recent development. In any case, the poor sufferer, the bed, and the cell were in an indescribable condition, and she herself had become more or less like an animal.

The thought of this Sister, lying in dirt and neglect was beyond Margaret's endurance. She went to the Prioress and asked leave to take care of her. After some hesitation, the Prioress agreed, but only on condition that she could persuade another nun to help her. Looking round her for someone whose courage she hoped might prove sufficient for the ordeal, her choice fell on Sister Alinka. Together, they went to the sick room, and Margaret went straight to the bedside.

'My dear Sister,' said she to the sick woman, 'have courage and do not lose patience.'

Then, stooping over the bed, alone she lifted the sick woman out and placed her on a chair. Sister Alinka said afterwards that she could not understand how the frail thin body of the Saint had stood up to the terrific strain. But poor Sister Alinka was not cast in the same heroic mold, and, even though she was only a bystander, the moving of the sick woman proved beyond her courage and shuddering she drew back. Margaret looked up from her task.

'My dear,' said she, 'since you cannot help me to do the work, go and leave me, for I can do it without you.'

In a mixture of shame and relief, Sister Alinka stepped back out of the room, but not out of sight; for she watched Sister Margaret clean and tidy the bed, put on fresh linen, and then lift the sick woman back. Again she was amazed at the supernatural strength which charity gave to the other. When the place was clean and tidy, Margaret gathered up all the soiled bed clothes, and carried them out to the river where she washed them. Her care of this sick sister did not cease until her death.

Doctors prescribed some very odd remedies in those days. A sister was suffering from a tumor, and the leech ordered a poultice of such an objectionable nature that not a sister in the house could face its preparation. Margaret came to the rescue at once. Alone she got the plaster ready and applied it to the sufferer.

The Saint's humility and the driving force of her vow had carried her very far, but she was not yet satisfied, for she did not yet feel that she had reached the place she had chosen and coveted under the feet of all. One way, a terrible way she saw, by which she could accomplish her desires and she took it.

The science of drainage and sanitation appears to have become a lost art for many centuries after the fall of the Roman Empire, hence one great reason for the frequent recurrence of the plague. Saint Mary of the Isle was fortunate in that it stood in the middle of a river, but such things as covered drains and drainage as we know it did not exist; the care of the sanitary condition of the house fell to the lot of a scavenger. Margaret constituted herself the scavenger, not only of the Priory, but of the adjacent huts. Then, at last, she was able to realize her ambition and fulfill her vow to the satisfaction of her own conscience; for she was now less than the least and under the feet of all.

No matter what the weather might be, her duties took her in and out frequently during the day, for she did her work thoroughly. Through mud, rain, and snow, backwards, and forwards she went, often plastered in mud to the knees, her delicate hands roughened and coarse, her nails broken and dirty; often enough she was a most disreputable sight. But she was more than carefree over the spectacle that she cut, she positively rejoiced in it. Her abjection was glorious in her own sight. Thus, and thus only, her loving heart rested content in that she was making to the full extent of her powers reparation for her country. The world has not seen many such patriots as Margaret of Hungary.

It was then that her Master came to her help and gave her her heart's desire. Sister Margaret was now, in a physical sense, a most unpleasant person with whom to come in contact, and many of the community avoided her. We can hardly blame them. But as Margaret noticed how she was shunned, her heart sang; that smile of hers of which her Acts tell us, swept over her face like sunshine.

She showed no resentment when she found herself so often left alone, though, as Divine Love does not kill but rather quickens human love, her sensitive nature must have suffered. Probably no one realized that she noticed she was being avoided, for people are apt to take living saints as a matter of course, and imagine that they feel no more than they show. Not long before her death, however, she made a remark which ought to have shown the community that, even if she were content to be left alone, she was not unaware of it. Some days before her death, while she was still perfectly well, she was speaking to a group of sisters and told them that on the feast of Saint Prisca she should die; going on to tell them where she would be buried. Then, with a spice of kindly malice, she added:

'You will no longer want to keep away from me then, for my body will be as fragrant after death as it is displeasing to you now.'

Such was Saint Margaret's active participation in reparation for her country; after her Consecration our Lord took the sacrificial knife into his own hand in order to make a perfect holocaust of this victim of love. Margaret began to witness what, to her human heart must have seemed like the utter failure of all her prayers and penances. Her brother Stephen rebelled against his father, and the very measures taken by Bela to repair the ruin which had been caused in his kingdom by the Tartars, led instead to civil wars, rebellion, and a partial paganization of the Magyar people.

Then Margaret's true agony began, her gethsemane. Boundless faith was asked of her in continuing her work of expiation, her prayers and her penances, although to all seeming God was deaf to her. Superhuman courage was required to carry on her hidden life of humiliation as if all were going well. That she persevered unflinchingly until death is in itself no small proof of the heroism of her sanctity.

In the very last year of her life, her father died, broken with grief at the death of his second, favorite and faithful son, Bela. She herself was called to her reward in the darkest hour when, humanly speaking, all things had gone awry. Remembering her loving human heart, her boundless devotion, and her utter unselfishness, it is possible to grasp to some extent the depth of her secret suffering.

Speaking of such a one, Blessed Henry Suso says:

'Thus, such a man's will is absolute in power, for heaven and earth serve him, and every creature is subject to him in what it does or leaves undone. He feels no sorrow of heart about anything; for pain and sorrow of heart are only caused by constraint of will. Externally he has a sense of pain and pleasure like others, and such is in him perhaps more intense because of his great tenderness; but in his inmost soul it finds no abiding place, and exteriorly, he remains firm against impatience. He is filled with joy even here below; for, being detached from self, his joy is complete.'

Chapter Seven

True love of God always leads to a love of mankind which is proportionate to the greater love. This love of the neighbor is not merely a sentiment of universal benevolence towards mankind in the mass; it is a personal, individual love of each and every soul which has been redeemed by the Precious Blood. Saint Margaret had a special love of and kindness towards every member of the human race.

In the first place, she was filled with deep devotion to the Church, and this devotion was a daily inspiration to fresh prayers and penances. The Popes were living in troublous times. The year after her birth, Innocent IV convoked the Council of Lyons, where the Emperor, Frederick IV, was cited for heresy, perjury, and sacrilege. A few years later, under Alexander IV, Ezzelino, Frederick's son-in-law, ravaged upper Italy so cruelly that there has not been, perhaps, since the world began, his equal for the refinement of tortures to which he subjected his unhappy victims. Italy was the battle ground of rival factions. Charles of Anjou, brother of Saint Louis of France, was invested by the Pope with the Kingdom of the Two Sicilies, from which he drove Manfred Hohenstaufen, of whom it was said: 'Never was an enemy so cruel to the Church.' Guelphs and Ghibelines divided the cities of Italy. Emperor and Pope were at mortal strife. In addition Tartar ravages were giving to the Church a host of martyrs.

Margaret heard with grief how monasteries were being destroyed and how monks and nuns were being driven out to combat with sickness and poverty in the world. It seemed to her that the cries and tears of the poor and innocent were calling to heaven for vengeance; and she wept and did penance for all who were being oppressed unjustly, redoubling her fasts and prayers to implore God to have mercy on the world. At times the nuns would grow weary of hearing Sister Margaret grieve with tears over the evils of the time, and would say to her:

'Why are you so grieved? All this does not touch you personally.'

'Is not the Church the Mother of all Christians?' Margaret would answer. 'This Mother of ours is being ferociously attacked, and her members are being snatched from her; and you ask me how this affects me personally? Am I not the child of Holy Mother Church? Is it not she who gave me birth and brought me into the world of Grace at the Baptismal font? And is it possible for the sorrows of this, my Mother, to leave me unmoved?'

Second only in intensity to her love of the Church was her love of her Order. Such a devotion was a tradition among the Hungarians, whose country had been one of the earliest cradles of the Order. In her case, there was yet another motive for love: remembering how great a part the Order of Preachers had played in the evangelization of eastern Europe, and recognizing how much Hungary herself owed to them, it was to Saint Dominic that Bela and Maria Lascaris had offered their unborn child in the time of their country's peril.

The period during which Saint Margaret lived was one both of glory and of trial for the

Order. The year in which she had been transferred to Saint Mary of the Isle, Saint Peter Martyr had suffered for the Faith in Verona, and Saint Thomas Aquinas had begun to preach in Paris. Three years after she had made Profession at Blessed Humbert's hands, Saint Hyacinth of Poland had died at Cracow; while in the year in which she had been Consecrated, 1260, the glorious Martyrs of Sandomir had suffered death at the hands of the Tartars while they sang the *'Salve Regina'* at Compline.

Troubles also pressed on the Friars, in great measure owing to the jealousy which their popularity with the people aroused. In the year in which Margaret took her Vows, Pope Innocent IV published a Bull depriving them of their privileges as preachers and confessors. This was not annulled until in 1255 when Pope Alexander IV published the Bull *Quasi Signum* which restored to the Friars all the privileges which Pope Honorious had granted to their Founder.

The Dominican nuns also had their troubles. The Friars complained that the care of the nuns involved them in work which they found incompatible with their office of preaching, and so they obtained, in 1252, a Bull removing the convents of nuns from the jurisdiction of the Master General and Provincials, and transferring them to the care of the bishops. This was a heavy blow to the nuns who had been given to the care of the Brethren by Saint Dominic himself. In 1255 the General Chapter was granted the right to consider requests made by individual convents; and these requests became so numerous, that finally, in 1267, under Blessed John of Vercelli, the right of jurisdiction was given back to the Order entirely.

Her love of her country and of her own family must often have made both of these the subjects of Margaret's most earnest prayers; and in both cases prayers were greatly needed. For one thing, as we have already said, Bela's domestic policy after the Tartars left the country in 1242, though excellent as a short time policy, was disastrous in the long run. In the first place, he gave the Cumans an enormous tract of the devastated land. Though he made it a condition that the settlers should embrace Christianity, in many cases this condition was unfulfilled; and even where the immigrants became nominal Christians, they remained pagan at heart. These settlers became, by reason of their numbers, a menace to the Christianity of Hungary.

In the second place, Bela encouraged the building of castle fortresses for the protection of the country, but these strongholds, under the control of the independent, rebellious nobles became merely centres of disaffection. The power of the king was thus, through the whole of his reign, hampered by two hostile forces, namely the native nobility and the pagan immigrants. There was a third hostile force, which found its storm centre in his own elder son.

Duke Stephen who, after his father's death, reigned for two troublous years as Stephen V, while he was still Crown Prince showed himself possessed of considerable ability, but restless, impatient of control, and violent. In 1262 he rebelled against his father, and in this connection an interesting story is told, which bears on the devotion of the royal family for the Friar Preachers.

The Master General of the Order, John the Teutonic, was, as we have already seen, a personal friend of both the King and the Queen. He died in 1252, and from that time on stories of the miracles that he was working constantly found their way to the then General, Blessed Humbert de Romans; to these Maria Lascaris added her testimony. She had been overwhelmed with grief because her husband and her son at the head of opposing armies were on the eve of battle, and her heart was torn between the love of her husband and of her child. So she prayed to John the Teutonic, begging him to prevent this dreadful civil war. As she prayed, he appeared to her, accompanied by Friar Gerard, a former Prior of the Order. The distracted Queen cried aloud to him:

'Give me back my son.'

Master John made the Sign of the Cross over her and said:

'I am giving you back your son.'

Next morning, a courtier came with the news that the King and his son were reconciled. Unfortunately the truce was only temporary. In 1263 Stephen again took up arms against his father. This time he actually fought and conquered the

King, forcing him to divide the Kingdom between the pair of them, by giving him twenty-nine counties in full sovereignty.

Bela died in 1269—two years before his daughter—on Saint Mary's Isle and was buried in the Priory Church. He was never reconciled to his son. On his death bed he gave the daughter, who was by his side, and his faithful followers orders to flee with the Crown Jewels to his grandson by marriage, Ottokar of Bohemia; a significant fact, since he and Ottokar had latterly been on anything but friendly terms.

The whole of Stephen's reign was comprised in two stormy years. His subjects considered him half a pagan, for he had married a Cuman princess, who, though she had been baptized before her marriage, still remained a pagan at heart, and she had great influence with her husband. Stephen died suddenly, a year after

Margaret, while he was in the act of raising an army to go to the rescue of his infant son, Ladislaus, who had been kidnapped by rebellious vassals. He also was buried in the Priory Church of Saint Mary of the Isle.

These fratricidal wars in which thousands of innocent men lost their lives caused Margaret such bitter sufferings that prayers and tears were her bread day and night. She knew that civil war of necessity brings in its train risk of eternal damnation, and she broke her heart to think that her father and brother should thus risk the loss of their souls. Moreover, in the last year of her life, when her brother Stephen was King, she endured an added sorrow, no less poignant for being a natural one, of seeing her family apparently doomed to destruction at the hands of the rebellious nobles.

Her preoccupation in world-wide intercession did not make Margaret forgetful of her own community; nor did her own sorrow, hidden from those with whom she came in contact lest they should be saddened by her, make her any less tender and compassionate towards all those who were in any grief or trouble often enough far lighter than those woes which saddened and oppressed her heart. She was gentle and kind to all, and in all things showed herself patient and long-suffering to anyone who wronged or offended her.

If she thought that a sister felt herself injured by anything that she might have said or done, Margaret would hasten to her and, making the *venia* at her feet, would humbly ask her pardon, promising to try to amend whatever she might have done amiss. If other nuns were angry or annoyed one with the other and the fact came to the Saint's ears, she never rested until she had healed the breach. It is said that her very presence brought peace in its train, and that there was never any discord where she happened to be. Sharp words died into silence as she came within earshot.

If by any chance she noticed that another sister had been avoiding her, and had not, perhaps, spoken to her for some days, she always sought her out and, prostrate before her, asked pardon, fearing lest she had inadvertently done something to wound her. It never entered her head that she might be the injured party, or that it was the duty of others to ask pardon of her. At the juridical inquiry into Saint Margaret's Cause, Sister Catherine made deposition that she saw the Saint once come to a member of the community who, for some reason or other, had not spoken to her for three days, and throwing herself humbly at the feet of the other, beg her pardon for any offence she might have given.

Suppose that she were to learn that any of the community were in grief for the sickness, death, or any other misfortune which had befallen any of their relations or friends, Margaret at once sought them out to share their sorrow with them and to do all in her power to comfort and strengthen them.

The poor were specially loved by her. Any gifts which were brought to her by relatives or friends were immediately, with the permission of the Prioress, distributed in alms; sometimes among the beggars who came to the Priory for food and clothing, sometimes to priests who worked among the poor, or to Churches situated in poor districts, where there was no one wealthy enough to help them. Father Marcellus, the Provincial, a prudent and holy man and her Spiritual Father, helped her in the distribution of alms. She was accustomed to exhort those who visited her to rule their subjects with justice, to oppress no one, to exercise charity towards the poor and widows, and to show mercy to all. Because of her great reputation as a servant of God, her exhortations did not go unheeded.

Sometimes, as she prayed near the Choir grille, she would notice some of the poor folk forced by infirmity to beg their livelihood in church porches. As soon as she saw one of these, she used to hasten to the Prioress and beg her to send out an alms.

Once in mid-winter, she came upon a poor beggar standing at the Priory door, her only clothing being a few poor rags. At once she ran to the Prioress and obtained leave to take off her best tunic, which she happened to be wearing—though considering her love of shabby clothing it can have been nothing very magnificent—in order to give it to the poor woman.

By order of the Prioress an extra dish called the Pittance used to be served to individual sisters who were considered to stand in need of it. If ever Margaret heard of one of the farm laborers falling sick, she used to ask leave to send her Pittance to the sick person. Sometimes her whole meal would follow the same path and she would rise fasting from the table.

She used to tell the younger nuns that the Vow of Poverty which had put it out of their power to give material alms, did not dispense them from this duty of charity. Whenever they saw anyone sick, poor or in trouble, they were under obligation to pray for such persons. This, she would add, is an alms of much greater value than any in money or in kind, such as they would have given in the world.

There was no lack of maimed beggars in those days, and they were wont to solicit sympathy and help by exposing their infirmities to the passers-by. When Margaret saw these poor folk, lame, blind, with withered limbs, or otherwise disfigured, she would weep from compassion, and would say to those about her:

'I am so sorry for these poor sick folk, and it grieves me that I cannot cure them. But at the same time I give thanks to the God who created me whole and sound in body and in limb, and who preserves me so even to this day. When I remember this, I feel all the more obliged to help those who are sick and poor. In particular I want to serve those who are ashamed of their poverty, and who hide themselves blushing lest it should be known. Those most of all do I wish to help.'

The alms of a man is as a signet with him; and shall preserve the grace of a man as the apple of his eye.

'And afterwards he shall rise up and shall render to them their reward, to every one upon their own head; and shall turn them down into the bowels of the earth'

(Ecclus: SVII, 18-19).

Chapter Eight

Being a true Dominican, Margaret was very simple in her life of prayer; she had no pet devotions, no minute rule of life, no complicated process by which she proposed to reach spiritual heights, the sort of process beginners find so seductive in its ingenious novelty. Her path lay plain and straight before her; by an instinct proper to the race of souls to which she belonged, as a true Dominican she seized on the most simple and the most fundamental facts of the spiritual life; for these are the most basic and the most elementary, and at the same time the highest and most doctrinal. She found no easy, sure path to Heaven; she followed the Blood-stained track left by her Spouse. Her Rule of Life was comprised in a maxim which had fallen in conversation from the lips of an old and experienced religious.

Father Marcellus, one time Provincial, and her Confessor, once told Saint Margaret that he prayed often and fervently to learn in what consisted the road to sanctity as it was followed by the holy, ancient Fathers, and which was so agreeable to God. In answer to his prayer he had the following vision. One night he was suddenly waked from sleep to seek a book before him written in letters of gold; and he heard a voice say:

'Friar, get up and read.' He obeyed, and found written on the page before him the following words:

THE WAY OF PERFECTION OF THE ANCIENT FATHERS IS THIS: TO LOVE GOD AND TO DESPISE YOURSELF: NOT TO JUDGE OR DESPISE ANYONE ELSE.

The Book of the Cross was Saint Margaret's only science. A wooden Cross sufficed to place always before her eyes the Mystery of the Blessed Trinity, and the entire economy of the Incarnation and Redemption. This was sufficient to spur her imperiously on to further love and sacrifice. With Saint Paul she might say: 'I do not count myself to have apprehended. But one thing I do; forgetting the things that are behind, and stretching myself to those that are before, I press towards the mark, the prize of the supernal vocation of God in Christ Jesus.'

Knowing that silence is the nurse of virtue, she loved silence, and when she had reason to speak was content with few words. She had a sense of humor—for without that she would never have made a saint—and a joyous nature. She was often seen to smile, but no one ever heard her break out in loud, unrestrained laughter. Above all things she hated to be praised, and all through her life no one ever heard from her lips the slightest boasting word.

One day, a young nun, speaking to Sister Helen Serrenj, expressed her surprise that Sister Margaret who worked so hard was so frail and delicate in appearance. Rather indiscreetly, Sister Helen made answer:

'If *you* always wore a hair shirt; if *you* were constantly taking or receiving the discipline; if *you* lived on bread and water; if *you* spent your whole nights in prayer; if *you* did all the penances that Sister Margaret does, then *you* would be just as frail as she is.'

These remarks eventually reached the ears of Sister Margaret herself, and she was much annoyed. Accordingly she went straight to the culprit and told her:

'Dear Sister, it was not right of you to talk about me in such a way. It was breaking confidence, and so, for the future, I shall tell you none of my secrets.'

Saint Margaret obeyed her Mistress, Sister Helen Olympiade, with admirable deference, in imitation of him who was obedient even to the death of the Cross. One day, in order to humiliate her, Helen said:

'Whatever sort of behavior do you call this of yours, Sister? You are always to be found on your knees, prostrate with your face to the earth like an animal. Is this the way that you seek in the dust for the Lord who is so high?'

Margaret only answered by a delightful smile.

She prayed all day and for the greater part of the night; indeed she prayed always, for what was her work but another form of prayer? Much of her time she spent before a Crucifix, and when her prayer was ended, she would lean forward, and with tears streaming down her cheeks would kiss the Five Wounds.

She was never idle, and disliked being interrupted during her prayer or work to see any of the royal or noble visitors who came to the Priory. True to her Dominican vocation, she had the greatest devotion to our Blessed Lady, whom she called 'my sweetest Hope and the Hope of the world.' She never heard her name pronounced whether by herself or by others, without falling on her knees and bowing down to the ground. Sister Catherine often used to ask her how to pray well, and the Saint's invariable answer was:

'Sister, offer God your soul and body; let your heart always cleave to him, so that neither death nor sorrow nor anything which happens here below, can separate you from him; this is to pray well.'

She was always most obedient. If the Prioress ever laid a command on all the community in general, she was ever the first to carry it out, and by her example she spurred on the rest. She never wished because of her royal rank to escape penances imposed on the community. It is on record that she once begged the Provincial to impose on her as on others the penance the Constitutions enjoined for deliberate breach of the very strict law of silence during meals.

The daily life of Saint Margaret seven hundred years ago is much the same as that lived by her enclosed Sisters today. At midnight the community was roused, and as soon as they were ready, the nuns recited the Matins of the Little Office of our Lady, standing in the Dormitory, unless the feast of the following day was above the rank of a Semi-double. Unlike the Great Office, the verses of the Psalms were recited alternately by the Hebdomadary and the community. When that was ended, all went to the Choir to sing Matins and Lauds. Lauds finished, the Martyrology was read in the Chapter Room and Pretiosa said. Then Chapter of Faults was held, at which the religious accused themselves, or were proclaimed by others of external breaches of Rule. The accusations took place after the Gospel, and before the Psalm *'Laudate'* of Pretiosa. After this the community returned to bed.

On rising in the morning, Prime and Tierce were sung; the Community Mass, Sext, and None followed at the appointed times. In a later century, perhaps to counteract the lessening of religious fervor, it was decreed that religious should give themselves to Mental Prayer twice daily, in the morning and in the evening. In the early days of the Order no such ordinance was necessary; as a matter of course, the religious gave themselves to long periods of silent prayer. As there were no periods set apart at that time for recreation, there was more free time to be employed in prayer.

Before each hour of the Canonical Office the appropriate Hour of the Little Office of our Lady was said in the cloister. In non-fasting seasons, dinner, the first meal of the day, was taken early, about eleven o'clock; during the time of the great fast, from the feast of the Exaltation of the Holy Cross until Easter, when there was only one meal in the day, this was not taken until between two and three o'clock in the afternoon.

Vespers were sung before sunset, and after that in non-fasting seasons there was a frugal supper. In fasting seasons the community assembled at the same time, and the Conferences of Cassian were read in the Refectory, while those who needed it took a cup of wine. No food of any kind was served. From this custom is derived the name of *collation* given to the evening meal in fasting seasons, for the Conferences of Cassian were called *'collationes.'* Compline was sung at night-fall; and after that the community went to their cells.

From her babyhood, Margaret had always loved prayer, and when only six years old, whenever she saw any nuns praying, she would run and join them. She was always first in Choir for Matins, nor, during the whole of her short life, was she ever absent from that Hour, from Mass, or from other Canonical Hours unless she were seriously ill. When she did lie down before Matins, which she did but seldom, before she rose again she crossed herself, and taking up her precious Crucifix with the relic of the True Cross, she kissed it with tears. Holding it before her so that she could see it, she would take it with her down to the grille in Choir, or to the Crucifix in the Chapter Room, where she would remain until the other nuns came down to Choir, unless Matins of our Lady was recited in the Dormitory. Matins ended, she was accustomed to remain in Choir praying until daybreak brought Prime and the Community Mass.

From thence on until dinner time she gave herself to prayer hearing as many Masses as she was able. She received Holy Communion according to custom, fifteen times in the year. On the whole of the day previous to her Communion she fasted rigorously and kept strict silence; the night she spent in vigil, humbling herself before God in prayer. The entire day on which she communicated was spent in thanksgiving; nor did she suffer food or drink to pass her lips before sun-down, when she took just sufficient to keep the life in her body. When the nuns communicated, it was customary for two of their number to hold the two ends of the Communion Cloth before the rest; it was Margaret's joy to be one of these sisters, so that she might look on her Lord again and again, as often as each received him.

Immediately after the midday meal, she straightway began her service of the sick and her domestic work. When she had finished she returned to prayer. After Compline, she remained in the Church until the doors were closed for the night; and this she would beg the sacristan to do as late as possible. When the doors were locked, she went to the Chapter Room and prayed before the Crucifix there, until the whole house was locked up for the night, after which she generally knelt by the side of her bed until shortly before midnight, when she roused the sister from whom she received the discipline. Before going to her cell, she made the round of the dormitory in case any sister was ill or in trouble; then if remedies were needed she provided them. No one knew if she went to bed or obtained the minimum of sleep necessary on the floor, because, as we have seen, she always took care to disturb her bed before going down stairs to Matins or Prime.

Margaret had her own ways of celebrating the greater feasts of the Church; although, perhaps, it is hardly correct to call them her own ways since they were also the ways of her Holy Father, Saint Dominic. The Dominican prostration is made by kneeling and bending the upper part of the body forward over the low bench in front of the stalls, or on the knees themselves when there are no stalls. On Christmas Eve, Margaret was accustomed to say a thousand *Paters* in honor of the Word made Flesh, prostrating anew for each *Pater*; on the vigil of

Pentecost she substituted a thousand times the *Veni Sancti Spiritus, reple tuoram corda fidelium*; while on the vigils of our Lady's feasts she said a thousand *Aves*. In this connection it is interesting to note that she only said the first part of the prayer, the second part not yet having been added.

One gathers from this that prayer was not a sweet and easy exercise to her. Once rapt in God, all movement would be a distraction if not an impossibility; whereas, if with a firm will to follow the right she adhered to God in spite of dryness, then she must of necessity force her body, half starved, always craving for sleep, and always in pain, to take its share in her prayer, otherwise prayer, as she understood it, would have been impossible. It was the only way in which at such times she could keep her attention; and it is in perfect keeping with the virile magnificence of her young life. Her knees, we are told, were broken and gnarled like the bark of an oak tree from kneeling, and her habit worn through at the knees and elbows from the number of prostrations that she made.

But prayer was not always hard and dry. Her cheeks were furrowed and discolored because of the tears that she shed in such abundance; her Lord in whose hands is the gift of infused contemplation did not suffer her fidelity to go unrewarded. Once several of the religious, when talking to her, suggested that she should shorten her prayers in order to lengthen her life, adding that in this way she would be able to merit longer.

She looked up with her usual delightful smile.

'Many of the people who look forward to a long life in this vale of tears,' she said, 'put off doing good works, since they think that they will have plenty of time before they die. As for me, I prefer to be of the number of those who, being anything but certain of a long life, consider that they have no time to lose if they wish to give God all the glory that they can before they die. Besides we all know that it is no more than a waste of time to live here in a convent if we are looking here for rest and comfort for our mortal body and for the joys of the world. The convent enclosure is a suitable home for those only who are seeking, not the perishable goods of this world but those which are eternal. For those only the convent is a true home.'

All through Lent, Margaret was occupied with the memory of the Passion, and as often as she could prevail on anyone to read the Gospel story to her, she listened intently and with tears. She suffered so acutely while the Passion was sung at the Mass on Palm Sunday that the nuns often feared that she would die then and there. During the fortnight before Easter Sunday she neither sat nor lay down, but remained the whole time either standing, kneeling, or prostrating.

She greatly loved to read the lives of her canonized ancestors, Saint Stephen, Saint Emericus, Saint Ladislaus, and her aunt Saint Elizabeth. It was in these that she centered her pride of race and lineage; she strove to emulate them and to come ever closer to God by copying their virtues. She had a great love, likewise, for the Martyrs, and longed to follow in their footsteps. She was often heard to say:

'How I wish that I had lived in the times of persecution so that I too might have been a martyr. O, why are there no persecutions in our own days, so that I might shed my blood for Christ? For his love I should rejoice to be burnt or beheaded, and so that the pain might last longer cut in pieces limb by limb, so that I might endure every kind of torment.'

Since her soul was drawn to heaven by her desires, it was but natural that her body should at times follow it. It frequently happened that on Good Friday, the Feast of All Saints, the Assumption, and many other feasts and vigils, she was seen raised more than a foot above the ground, and there she would remain for a long time, while she became as one dead, deprived of the use of her senses and of all power of motion.

One vigil of All Saints, while she was praying, she suddenly fell and lay like one dead, remaining thus while Sister Helen the younger, who was praying with her, said the whole Psalter. It was not the first time that Sister Helen had seen her in ecstasy, but now she remained in that state for so long motionless and without appearing even to breathe, that her companion began to think that she must in truth be dead; and so, between grief and shock, she lost her head and started to cry out and make a great commotion. Then, seeing that her cries and tears effected nothing, she ran out and called the community who all hurried to the spot, to find Sister Margaret lying there to all appearance dead. Hardly, however, had the last sister arrived when Sister Margaret returned to herself. She looked round on the frightened weeping nuns with much surprise.

'My Sisters' she said, 'why are you so disturbed? It is true that I lost consciousness a moment ago, but it was for such a short while, that there was no cause for alarm.'

Once, when she was praying one of the community called her seven times, but she heard nothing; at the eighth repetition, she answered as though it was the first time that she had been called. Often when she returned to herself after prayer she seemed so beautiful and majestic that her sisters hardly dared look at her.

In Saint Margaret then we have examples of two kinds of prayer; that of the will carried on in spite of weariness and heaviness of the bodily powers, and the prayer of infused contemplation, when the Master himself takes the soul and raises it up. 'I live, now not I, but Christ liveth in me.'

Once, during Advent when she was spending the night in prayer, she was suddenly rapt in ecstasy, and a flame of fire appeared over her head. The nun who was with her, again Sister Helen the younger, called her several times, and since she did not answer, the young nun, who does not appear to have got accustomed to the Saint's ecstasies, or to have lost her fear of them, ran to the Choir where she found several more of the community praying. They came at once, and all saw the marvel which so ravished them with its beauty that they remained a long time watching. Several times they tried to attract Sister Margaret's attention, but being in ecstasy she could neither see nor hear them.

At last she returned to herself slowly and half dazed as though she had been roused from a deep sleep. The nuns, excited and vociferous, all began to tell her that there was a flame resting on her head. Margaret, who by this time was completely herself again, quietly lifted her hand to her head, and the flame disappeared. She begged those present to say nothing about the occurrence; but she could not hide the delicious perfume which filled the air, and hung about the place for a long time afterwards.

The flame of divine love burned so ardently in her soul that material fire seemed to have no power over her. Once, when she came into the kitchen she found the cook in great tribulation. The tripod which held the great iron pot over the fire had slipped. The contents of the pot had caught fire, and both that and the tripod were red hot. There was real danger of a conflagration, but no one knew what to do, for they could not reach the pot in the middle of the fire, neither could they have touched it if they had been able to reach it.

Saint Margaret quietly put her hand right into the fire, gripped the pot and the tripod and lifted the former to safety. There was no sign, or even smell of burning either on her hand or on her arm.

Chapter Nine

The whole tenor of her life leads us to suppose that almost as a matter of course Saint Margaret worked miracles.

In reading or hearing about the miracles worked by the saints, one is apt to concentrate with disproportionate interest on the extraordinary and preternatural element that they necessarily contain. This is very understandable, since it is this element which appeals to our sense of wonder; though if we look at the matter dispassionately, it is not really extraordinary, after all, that these servants of God, who have conquered their own sin-weakened natures, should be given command likewise of external nature. The element which is really of the deepest interest in studying miracles lies in their revelation of the psychology of the saint who works them; and those worked by Saint Margaret certainly give us an insight into her character from another angle.

In every other phase of her life, she shows herself to us as one endowed with the use of reason from infancy, possessed of wisdom from her youth; all her life long exhibiting an old head on young shoulders. Her miracles show her to us in her youth and joyousness, for she was only twenty-eight years old when she died, possessed of a certain care-free comradeship with Almighty God—I use the expression in all reverence. She had given him her all, and in return he treated her as his spoilt child, and she almost seems to expect this.

When she was only ten, she went one dark overcast day into the Infirmary, to find some children playing there. The room was very dark, for medieval windows were no more than unglazed slits, and unless the weather were really bright outside the interior of the house was always gloomy. So the children could not see what they were doing. Perhaps, too, after the fashion of children some of them were afraid of the dark; one or two of them may have been whimpering. Margaret came up to them and said:

'Would you like me to make the sun shine in here for you?' the children agreed that this would be very pleasant, but it was, of course, a thing that neither she nor anyone else could do.

'Do you see that corner over there?' she pointed with her finger. 'Well, I will go over there for a while, and presently I will come back to you.

Now while I am away you will see the sun shining brightly.'

She walked over to the appointed spot, quite close at hand but just out of sight, and began to pray. Immediately the sun appeared, shining through the Infirmary windows, and lighting up the whole place, until Margaret had ended her prayer and returned to them.

She always got on well with children and they were not afraid of taking liberties with her. Her niece, Sister Elizabeth, daughter of Stephen V, had been brought up from babyhood at Saint Mary's Isle. There had been many discussions between the children as to whether or not Sister Margaret always wore a hair shirt. One day, her niece determined to ascertain the facts of the case for herself. Accordingly, while standing by her aunt, she somehow contrived to slip her hand down between her shoulders. In this way the child settled the matter to her own satisfaction, as she deposed at the Process, but not at all to that of her aunt, who drew back much embarrassed, saying:

'Leave me alone, child. Now, run away quickly.'

One day she and another nun were carrying a batch of unbaked bread on a large flat tin covered with a cloth across the garden to the bakehouse. There was a heavy gale of wind blowing; in fact, it was so strong that it had already lifted the roof of the Chapter Room and carried it bodily over to the orchard. When the two had gone some part of the distance, they found themselves so exposed to the fury of the wind that Margaret's companion was terrified and wished to return. But Margaret would have none of it.

'We will just stand here and pray,' said she, 'God will help us.' As they prayed the wind suddenly died down and they completed their journey in perfect calm.

Three of the miracles worked by Saint Margaret are not unlike that told of Saint Scholastica and Saint Benedict; and they certainly show her possessed of a delightful sense of humor.

One of the Friars came to the Priory to preach. The community invited him to stop the night and give them a second sermon next day. The Friar refused; he had work to do and could not spare the time. Leaving the parlor, he went in search of his horse and trap, for Bela had evidently connected Saint Mary of the Isle with the mainland by a bridge. Margaret was very anxious for him to remain; when, however, she saw that he was determined to go, she made no comment but betook herself to prayer.

When the Friar reached his trap it was to find that the vehicle was broken and unusable. On making wrathful inquiries he was assured that no one had touched it. There was nothing else to be done but to make the best of a bad job, go back to the Priory for the night and gives the nuns the sermon they had asked for. He must also have had a sense of humor, and he had made a good guess as to the cause of the mishap, for next morning, when his exhortation was ended, turning to Margaret, he said:

'You have forced me to do what you wanted, Sister; now you must give me back my trap.'

Margaret still said nothing, but betook herself again to prayer and straightway the vehicle was found completely repaired, though no one had been near it since the previous day.

The same thing happened to another Friar who refused to stay and preach a second sermon; only in this case, the victim had gone some distance before the break-down of his cart forced his return.

On a third occasion when a like request had been refused, Margaret said that she would pray for such a down-pour of rain as should force him to return; and this is what actually happened.

One miracle was worked by her because her veracity had been called in question. Margaret had been relating to the Provincial and a group of sisters some circumstances connected with an inundation of the Danube that she had seen. The Provincial refused to believe her; he told her that it was impossible for anything of the sort to have occurred, and that she must have imagined it. Margaret was angry, for to call her veracity in question in this way was to cast a doubt on her honor as a Dominican; and she gloried in belonging to the Order of Truth.

'My God, I beg of you to show that I am speaking the truth,' she cried.

Immediately the waters of the Danube began to rise, overflowing the river banks. Swiftly rose the river, and soon the community were driven from the shore where they had been standing back to the Priory. Still the water continued to rise until the whole ground floor of the building was submerged, and the nuns were obliged to retire to the upper part of the house.

The Provincial, somewhat perturbed, climbed the enclosure wall, and from this point of vantage watched the flood still rising. Then the nuns gathered around Margaret, begging her to undo the mischief she had done. This she was quite willing to do now that the veracity of her statement had been proved. So she prayed again, and the waters immediately began to subside. The inundation had begun just after Vespers, and by Matins the river was again flowing smoothly between its banks; and more wonderful still, it had carried its mud back with it leaving no trace whatsoever of the flood.

It happened one Easter Eve that Margaret sent one of the serving maids, a certain Sister Agnes, out to the garden to fetch her tunic which was drying there. All those employed in the Priory delighted to serve the Saint, well pleased of the opportunity of making some little return for all that she did for them; so this girl ran out into the dusk of a rainy evening without bothering to look where she was going. Crossing the courtyard at a headlong pace, she fell into the deep well from which the community drew their supply of water.

After some time, as she did not return, the nuns and other serving maids went out in search of her. Eventually the broken curb of the well gave them a clue, and after a good deal of purposeless running hither and thither, someone went for the Saint. Immediately she hurried out, and falling prostrate by the well, covering her face with her veil, with outstretched, joined hands, she began to pray; for she was much distressed to think that the accident had happened in her service. Then the bystanders saw the body of the girl appear on the surface of the water, but the limbs were contorted, and she was to all appearance quite dead.

In the meantime, the Portress came to say that some of the Friars were at the gate, and a message was immediately sent asking their help. Hurrying to the scene, they procured a ladder, and descended the well, while Margaret remained absorbed in prayer. With much difficulty they succeeded in bringing the body out which they laid on the ground, to all appearance lifeless. Margaret again set herself to prayer and straightaway the maid arose alive and perfectly healed, to throw herself at the Saint's feet and thank her for her restoration. She lived for several years after this.

There was a certain nun who was seriously ill in the Infirmary, and no remedies seemed to give her any relief. Margaret came to see her and being full of compassion for her sufferings began to make inquiries as to whether there was anything which had not yet been tried. When she learnt that there was a remedy which no one had yet used for her, the Saint went off, procured it, and took it to the invalid. The sick sister was evidently very anxious to get well, and, according to modern notions, must have been a highly nervous patient, for as soon as Sister Margaret showed her what she had brought, she became so excited and anxious that she grew rapidly worse. Before long aphasia set in, and those with her feared that she would lose her reason as well as her speech.

Margaret was grief-smitten, agonized to think that what she had hoped would be an occasion of her restoration to health should prove to be in reality the means of her death. She could not leave the patient, so she sent another nun who was standing by to bring her case of relics, and in particular her own relic of the True Cross. Kneeling down, and stretching out her clasped hands, she prayed with many tears:

'My Lord, Jesus Christ, if you will permit me, your unworthy handmaid to beseech your Divine Majesty, and if my prayer is pleasing to you, show me this mercy, and grant me this, that your sick servant by the wealth of your loving kindness, may be brought back to health.'

As soon as Margaret's prayer was ended, the sick sister sat up in bed, fully restored to health, as she herself afterwards testified.

Once in the presence of Sister Margaret, one of her nieces, the Saint restored the use of her limbs to a paralyzed woman. At another time, Sister Agatha, watching by the bedside of a sick nun, saw the Saint enter her cell. Going up to the sick sister she said to her:

'Dear Sister, get up at once, for you are quite well again.' The nun instantly rose from her bed, completely cured.

Sister Maria told how once the Saint had a badly swollen shoulder. How painful it was can be guessed from the fact that she went to the Infirmary. The Infirmarian was busy in applying remedies (for Sister Margaret was so kind to the sick that she rejoiced to have an opportunity of serving her) when another nun came into the room. Something must have happened to upset the newcomer's temper, for she at once began to rail at the Saint, telling her that she was making a commotion about nothing. Immediately the scoffer was conscious of a severe pain in her own shoulder, which at once began to swell up just as Sister Margaret's had done. It did not take her long to realize that in punishment of her mockery she was being made to know the reality of Sister Margaret's suffering; so, straightway acknowledging her fault and asking pardon, the nun was instantly cured of both pain and swelling.

Once a nun came to the Saint with a badly swollen finger to ask her if she had a medicinal ring to ease the pain. Taking the sufferer's hand in her own, she twisted her own finger round the other's swollen one, making as it were a ring of it, and she was cured at once.

Brother John, a Lay Brother from the Priory at Spalato, a good man and a devoted religious, was taken ill with a quartern ague which lasted from the feast of Saint Dominic to that of the Purification. This ague appears to have been a kind of malaria which rendered the sufferer quite prostrate while it lasted, but gave him intervals when he could go about and live a normal life. The bouts of fever had so weakened Brother John that no doctor could do him any good, though all were agreed that if no cure could be found he must very soon die.

He as a very useful man to the Provincial who took him as his companion on most of his journeys, so, being very loath to lose him, he sent the Brother to Saint Margaret to ask for a cure.

Brother John came to the Turn and asked to see the Saint, who with her accustomed humility and obliging manner came at once.

'Your Spiritual Father, Father Marcellus the Provincial,' said Brother John, 'has sent me to you that you may pray for me and deliver me from approaching death through this ague which is troubling me.'

Margaret was silent for a little while, deliberating within herself, then at last she answered:

'Jesus Christ is our Master who puts sickness to flight and gives us life and health. I will do what I can as my Spiritual Father has commanded; but you must pray likewise.'

Then she went to the little Oratory which was her place of prayer outside the Choir, between the walls of the Choir and those of the Church. There she prayed secretly before the Crucifix and the pictures of the Saints which were there and which it was her joy to tend. Meanwhile the sick man returned home; but on the day when his fever was wont to come on him, he remained in perfect health, nor did the fever ever return, thanks to her intercession. Many of the friars testified to Brother John's long illness and its cure.

Saint Margaret possessed the gift or prophecy and the kindred gift of reading hearts. Sister Petronilla, a novice of high lineage and great wealth, was standing at Collation one day, when she happened to notice how shabby her habit was and how poorly she was dressed.

She gave the thought house-room, and by the end of the reading, she was thoroughly discontented with life as it was and was even toying with the temptation to return home. Novices in those days were not kept separate from the Professed Sisters as they are now, so after they had left the Refectory, Margaret sought her out and began to speak thus:

'Yes, my dear Sister, it is true that you are lovely, and you may be as pleased with yourself as you like in your beautiful habit, so give no more heed to these empty thoughts, and cease to waste your time on such rubbish.'

The abashed Petronilla understood that her temptation had been made known to Margaret, and, promising to think no more about returning to the world, she humbly asked the Saint to pray for her perseverance.

Sister Alinka had lost her appetite, and as she sat at table, looking with some disgust at the plain fare, and thinking to herself that she needed some sort of pick-me-up to restore her appetite, the temptation came to her: 'If I were not a Religious and were at home at table with my parents, when they saw that I was indisposed like this how many of the servants would be bustling around me, bringing all manner of cordials to tempt my appetite.' So she sat, playing with the temptation, feeling herself a very ill-used person indeed. After supper, she did not go out of the Refectory with the others, but remained in her place, feeling thoroughly depressed. After the community had returned from Choir, Sister Margaret came to her:

'Dear Sister, what is the matter with you?' she asked.

'You see very well what is the matter with me,' answered Alinka rather crossly, for she felt in no mood for Sister Margaret's admonitions.

Then said Margaret to her: 'Is it such a small thing that you are thinking of leaving the Order, or are regretting that you are a religious?'

Sister Alinka was touched by grace and put the dangerous thoughts out of her mind; but so ashamed was she to think that her beloved Sister Margaret had read her heart, that for three days she could not look her in the face. The matter did not end here. When the juridical inquiry was opened, Sister Alinka was still so ashamed of herself that she decided to say nothing about the way in which her thoughts had been read by the Saint. But the poor religious was not to get off so lightly. She was taken ill, and realizing that this was in punishment for her cowardice, she told the story of her temptation and its cure in full, and was immediately restored to health.

Another nun, Sister Catherine, had been very much put out. Quite probably she had cause for annoyance, but as she sat at table, she nursed her feelings of bitterness, and began to plan a petty revenge. But, knowing that she was within view of Sister Margaret, she was careful to keep the expression of her face serene and pleasant. After Grace, however, Margaret waited for her and asked her what she was thinking of during dinner. Said Sister Catherine, somewhat disconcerted, but determined to brazen the matter out:

'What was I thinking of? Why, I was eating and thinking of the food; what else should I be thinking of?'

Then the Saint with great gentleness and sweetness, told her in detail all she was thinking of. Sister Catherine must have been a good and humble soul at bottom, for she owned that Margaret had read her thoughts, and thanked her for her sisterly help.

One evening the Saint and an old religious were watching by the body of a member of the community who had lately died. The old nun as she knelt by the bier was recalling her own age, and saying how it would be her turn to follow the other before long. Margaret turned to her and said sweetly:

'My dear Mother, it is I who will die first. And I shall be buried at the foot of the Altar of the Holy Cross.'

More than a year before her death she foretold the day on which she was to die. We have already recounted how some days before her death, though she was still in her normal state of health, she told the Prioress and some of the older sisters that death was imminent.

'I shall die,' she said, 'on the feast of Saint Prisca.' And this fell out exactly as she had foretold.

Chapter Ten

On January 5th, Margaret was attacked with so violent a fever that she was obliged to go to bed. As the day passed and she grew steadily worse, news of her illness was sent to all the other Monasteries and Convents within reach, to ask for prayers. As soon as the tidings came to the Dominican Priory, Father Michael, the Provincial, came with Father Marcellus, the ex-Provincial and the Saint's Confessor. The latter heard her Confession, and gave her Holy Viaticum at once. She asked to receive Extreme Unction also, and her request was granted. Although in a high fever she never became delirious, but retained to the last the full control of her senses.

As the end drew near she asked that the nuns might come to her cell so that she could say good-bye to them. This she did with the greatest joy, for eternal union with her Spouse was near. She exhorted the nuns to love of God and contempt of the world; telling them of the reward that their sweet Spouse, Jesus, reserves for those who are united to him through life with all their strength of will.

Then turning to Sister Elizabeth, the Prioress, she handed her the key of the box in which, she said, she kept her greatest treasures. When it was opened after her death, it was found to contain two hair shirts, and an iron girdle two fingers in width, the belt made of hedgehog skins, her disciplines, and other instruments of penance.

Having thus made an end of all that concerned her dealings with others, the rest of the time which elapsed before her death was passed in converse with her Lord. She appears to have suffered but little; perhaps her Spouse was in this way making her a return for all that she had voluntarily endured during her life for his sake. As her mind was clear and alert, so her poor wasted body was sweet and wholesome. She was free, so her Life tells us, from all corruption of body or mind.

So she lay until January 18th, and as the time for which she longed drew nearer, so did her desires and yearning become stronger. With Saint Paul, she desired to be dissolved and to be with Christ. Then, on the thirteenth day of her sickness, surrounded by a number both of friars and of nuns, she gave up her pure soul to her Creator, in the twenty-ninth year of her age.

After her death her face glowed with a wonderful light and beauty. From under their closed lid, her eyes shone with a marvelous golden glow, showing even in her body the glory of her resurrection. They carried her holy remains to the Church, and there they remained four days unburied, because of the great concourse of people who crowded to gaze on her wondrous beauty, and to beg her intercession.

On the day after her death, the Archbishop of Esztergom came with a company of his chief clergy. The sorrowing nuns accompanied him to the Church, where he gazed long on the child whom he had baptized, confirmed, and whose Solemn Consecration as a Virgin he had received. Then turning to the weeping sisters, he said:

'My children, you should not weep for this daughter of the Eternal King; let us rather rejoice, because we can see that she has manifestly received the reward of Eternal Life.'

At the end of four days a paving stone before the High Altar was raised and the body of the Saint was laid to rest there, in the presence of the Archbishop and many of her own Brethren, as well as the Friars Minor and the Premonstratensian Canons. There was a vast crowd of people, both nobles and commons, rich and poor, praising God for the glory that he showed in his servant. After the ceremony the tomb was left uncovered, and the body of the Saint exhaling a sweet fragrance, was left for all to see, though a veil covered her face. After the grave had remained open for several days, it was covered with a plain stone. Three months later it was again opened that the stone might be replaced by a marble tomb; and again the wonderful perfume was perceptible to all.

Many wonders immediately preceded and followed her death, presaging the glory that was to be hers. A few days before her death, a Premonstratensian Canoness, of the Monastery of Saint Michael also on Saint Mary's Isle, had a vision in which she saw our Lady accompanied by a great host of Saints and Angels, carrying in her hand a rich crown. She descended to the Dominican Priory, and there the nun saw her enter the cell of the Virgin Margaret. Standing before her, our Blessed Lady crowned her with the crown of inestimable brightness and beauty which she carried. Then there appeared a shining ladder reaching from the cell to heaven, and taking Margaret with them the heavenly company ascended the steps until they were lost to sight. This in very truth happened but a few days later.

Another nun of the same Order, living in a Monastery at Pesth, saw a brilliant light like a star going up to heaven at the moment of the Saint's death. She asked the Angels whom she saw hovering round what this might mean, and they replied:

'It is Margaret, the daughter of King Bela, who has left earth for heaven.'

On the night of her death, Friar Peter, a Lector in a Dominican Priory, while he was sleeping after Matins, heard a voice saying:

'The Lamb is dead.'

Next morning, when he arose, he told the other Friars what he had heard. They all agreed that it could mean nothing else than that Margaret was dead. So they sent a messenger to the Priory to find that such was indeed the case.

This same Friar also experienced her healing power. He was suffering from a bad abscess under a tooth. The pain was intense, and in consequence he had not slept for four nights. On the fifth night since the pain was as severe as ever, he asked Sister Margaret to obtain a cure for him, promising in return to genuflect every day in her honor. He was immediately cured.

On the night of the Saint's death, the passing of Sister Margaret's spirit was shown to a woman, a matter-of-fact person to whose word credence might safely be given, and who lived between twenty-six and twenty-nine miles away from the Priory. When she got up next morning, she went to the master of the house, an honorable man and one of the nobility and said to him:

'Though I have not heard anything about it, I know that the Lady Margaret, the nun daughter of King Bela is dead; for last night I saw her taken up to heaven in glory, and she said to me: "Let those who desire to have their sins pardoned, hasten to my tomb, and there they shall receive pardon from God."'

All through that day, which was a Sunday, the master of the house refused to believe the tale. When evening came, however, he decided to ride over to the Priory to find out for himself the truth of the woman's story. There he learnt that the previous evening the Lady Margaret had indeed gone to God and that they were even then taking her body to the Church. Full of wonder, the man told the assembled Friars exactly what had happened.

A Friar named Romanus died shortly before Saint Margaret. Soon after her death he appeared to his Prior to beg the Friars to offer Masses for him, and to remember him in their prayers, for he was in Purgatory. The Prior said to him:

'What is the state of the Lady Margaret who died three weeks ago?'

'She had gone up to heaven,' said the dead Friar, 'clothed in golden robes adorned with many jewels.'

And now our Holy Father the Pope has himself set the seal of the Church on the Cult of Saint Margaret. In the Decretal Letter he says: 'In this report he (Cardinal Rossi) most amply showed that it was evident concerning the holiness of the life of Blessed Margaret; and concerning the virtues practiced by her in a heroic degree; of which virtues her charity and love of prayer and severe penance were conspicuous; concerning the cult shown to the blessed one either by the people from the day of her death even to our own time or by the liturgical cult approved by the Apostolic See; concerning the fame of the miracles, whereby she is honored... Wherefore, after maturely considering all things, with certain knowledge, by the plenitude of Our

Apostolic Power…We solemnly decree: That the Blessed Margaret, of the royal family of the Arpads, a nun of the Order of Saint Dominic, is a Saint and is to be enrolled in the calendar of the Saints…

'So, therefore, the memory of this newly admitted Saint having been consecrated by Us, We trust that she will indeed resume her mission of propitiatory victim before God, not only for her beloved native land which is deservedly held to be a bulwark of the Catholic Faith and the Christian name, but also for all the nations at present waging war so bitterly among themselves; and that by her continual and potent prayers she may obtain from the most loving Lord, "the Father of Mercies and the God of all consolations" for mankind drawn to the sweet yoke of the Gospel, a tranquility and a peace founded firmly on the justice and charity of Christ.'

About the Author

Sister Mary Catherine Anderson, O.P. was born Kathleen Agnes Cicely Anderson on January 21, 1888 in Falmouth, Cornwall, England. Born to an Anglican clergyman, Kathleen converted with her family to the Catholic Church when still a little girl. She was educated by the Stone Dominican Sisters at their convent of St. Marychurch and entered the congregation on May 2, 1908 at St. Dominic's Convent, Stone, receiving the religious name of Sister Mary Catherine. Sister made her profession on November 25, 1909 and afterwards trained as a primary school teacher at the Sacred Heart Training College in St. Charles's Square, London.

By 1936, when Sister was assigned to St. Marychurch, she had begun to write—mainly historical novels of the revolts in Devon and

Cornwall. It was during this time that Sister wrote her most popular book, *Brother Petroc's Return,* which received great acclaim in both England and America. Following this came many other titles including two biographies—*Steward of Souls* and *A Treasure of Joy and Gladness*—as well as lives of St. Margaret of Hungary and of St. Hyacinth.

After her retirement she was appointed prioress to the community in Kelvedon, Essex and then assigned to the convent in Brewood where she continued to write. She died at Stone on April 14, 1972 in the 85th year of her life and the 63rd year of religious profession.

Made in the USA
Charleston, SC
19 March 2014